Science

Science

Ferguson's

An Infobase Learning Company

Discovering Careers: Science

Copyright © 2011 by Infobase Learning

Ferguson's
An imprint of Infobase Learning
132 West 31st Street
New York NY 10001

Library of Congress Cataloging-in-Publication Data

Science. — 1st ed.
    p. cm. — (Discovering careers)
Includes bibliographical references and index.
ISBN-13: 978-0-8160-8053-3 (hardcover : alk. paper)
ISBN-10: 0-8160-8053-4 (hardcover : alk. paper) 1. Science—Vocational guidance—Juvenile literature. I. Ferguson Publishing.
Q147.S27 2011   500—dc22
                          2010042278

Ferguson's books are available at special discounts when purchased in bulk quantities for businesses, associations, institutions, or sales promotions. Please call our Special Sales Department in New York at (212) 967-8800 or (800) 322-8755.

You can find Ferguson's on the World Wide Web at
http://www.infobasepublishing.com

Text design by Erik Lindstrom and Erika K. Arroyo
Composition by Erika K. Arroyo
Cover printed by Bang Printing, Brainerd, MN
Book printed and bound by Bang Printing, Brainerd, MN
Date printed: March 2011

Printed in the United States of America

10 9 8 7 6 5 4 3 2 1

This book is printed on acid-free paper.

CONTENTS

Introduction

You may not have decided yet what you want to be in the future. And you don't have to decide right away. You do know that right now you are interested in science. Do any of the statements below describe you? If so, you may want to begin thinking about what a career in science might mean for you.

_____ Science is my favorite subject in school.
_____ I like to do science experiments.
_____ I like animals/plants/insects.
_____ I collect rocks.
_____ I collect specimens to view under my microscope.
_____ I like to study dinosaurs.
_____ I spend a lot of time working with my chemistry set.
_____ I like looking at the stars through my telescope.
_____ I am concerned about the environment.
_____ I am fascinated by earthquakes/volcanoes/tornadoes.
_____ I am curious about how things work.
_____ I am good at observing small details.
_____ I like to solve problems.
_____ I like to learn about the ocean.
_____ I am good at math.
_____ I like to take things apart and see if I can put them back together again.
_____ I like to invent things.

Discovering Careers: Science is a book about careers in science, from agricultural scientists to zoologists. Scientists help us learn about our universe. Some scientists make discoveries about the Earth, sky, atmosphere, animals, plants, and people. Other scientists figure out practical ways to use those discoveries to make our lives better.

This book describes many possibilities for future careers in the sciences. Read through it and see how different science careers are connected. For example, if you are interested in animals, you will want to read the chapters on agricultural scientists, biologists, marine biologists, and zoologists. If you are interested in the Earth, you will want to read the chapters on geologists, geophysicists, ecologists, oceanographers, and soil scientists. Perhaps you're interested in stargazing. If so, you should read the article on astronomers. Go ahead and explore!

What Do Scientists Do?

The first section of each chapter begins with a heading such as "What Astronomers Do" or "What Chemists Do." It tells what it's like to work at this job. It describes typical responsibilities and assignments. You will find out about working conditions. Which scientists work in laboratories? Which ones work outside in all kinds of weather? What tools and equipment do they use? This section answers all these questions.

How Do I Become a Scientist?

The section called "Education and Training" tells you what schooling you need for employment in each job—a high school diploma, training at a junior college, a college degree, or more. It also talks about on-the-job training that you could expect to receive after you're hired and whether or not you must complete an apprenticeship program.

How Much Do Scientists Earn?

The "Earnings" section gives the average salary figures for the job described in the chapter. These figures provide you with a general idea of how much money people with this job can make.

Keep in mind that many people really earn more or less than the amounts given here because actual salaries depend on many different things, such as the size of the company, the location of the company, and the amount of education, training, and experience you have. Generally, but not always, bigger companies located in major cities pay more than smaller ones in smaller cities and towns, and people with more education, training, and experience earn more. Also remember that these figures are current averages. They will probably be different by the time you are ready to enter the workforce.

What Will the Future Be Like for Scientists?

The "Outlook" section discusses the employment outlook for the career: whether the total number of people employed in this career will increase or decrease in the coming years and whether jobs in this field will be easy or hard to find. These predictions are based on economic conditions, the size and makeup of the population, foreign competition, and new technology. They come from the U.S. Department of Labor, professional associations, and other sources.

Keep in mind that these predictions are general statements. No one knows for sure what the future will be like. Also remember that the employment outlook is a general statement about an industry and does not necessarily apply to everyone. A determined and talented person may be able to find a job in an industry or career with the worst kind of outlook. And a person without ambition and the proper training will find it difficult to find a job in even a booming industry or career field.

Where Can I Find More Information?

Each chapter includes a sidebar called "For More Info." It lists organizations that you can contact to find out more about the field and careers in the field. You will find names, addresses, phone numbers, and Web sites of science-related associations and government agencies.

Extras

Every chapter has a few extras. There are photos that show scientists in action. There are sidebars and notes on ways to explore the field, lists of recommended personal and professional qualities, fun facts, profiles of people in the field, and lists of Web sites and books that might be helpful.

At the end of the book you will find three additional sections: "Glossary," "Browse and Learn More," and "Index." The Glossary gives brief definitions of words you may be unfamiliar with that relate to education, career training, or employment. The Browse and Learn More section lists science-related books, periodicals, and Web sites to explore. The Index includes all the job titles mentioned in the book.

It's not too soon to think about your future. We hope you discover several possible career choices. Happy hunting!

Agricultural Scientists

What Agricultural Scientists Do

Agricultural scientists study plants and animals in their environments. They conduct research in laboratories or in the field. They use the results of their research to increase crop yields and improve the environment. Sometimes they plan and set up programs to test foods, drugs, and other products. They may be in charge of activities and public exhibits at such places as zoos and botanical gardens. Agricultural scientists teach at colleges and universities. Some work as advisers to business firms or the government. Others work in technical sales and service jobs for companies that make agricultural products.

Many agricultural scientists, wherever they work, concentrate on some type of scientific research. They work either with a team of scientists or agricultural engineers. The head of a research project is usually someone with a doctoral degree (Ph.D.) in agricultural science. The staff working on the research project can range from students to people with advanced degrees.

Agricultural scientists called *agronomists* try to find the causes of major food-crop problems. They research plant diseases, pests, and weeds and also study soil. Their goal is to improve the nutrition, hardiness (health), and taste of the plants by finding better ways to manage disease and soil conditions on the farm.

Scientists called *horticulturists* study the genes and the physical elements of plants to figure out ways to improve them. They try to make flowers, vegetables, fruits, and nuts grow faster, bigger, and more resistant to disease by producing better genetic strains of the plants.

EXPLORING

- Visit Web sites to learn more about agricultural science. Here are a few suggestions: *Careers in Agronomy: Growing Your Future* (https://www.agronomy.org/files/career-brochures/asa-career-brochure.pdf), Farm Service Agency: Kids (http://www.fsa.usda.gov/FSA/kidsapp?area=home&subject=landing&topic=landing), and *Grow Your Future* (https://www.crops.org/files/career-brochures/cssa-career-brochure.pdf).
- Joining the National FFA Organization (http://www.ffa.org) or 4-H (http://4-h.org) will give you a chance to work with others on agricultural projects, such as raising livestock or crops. Contact your county's extension office to learn about research projects in your area.
- Visit zoos, agricultural laboratories, greenhouses, or plant nurseries to explore the many opportunities available to agricultural scientists. You may be able to volunteer at zoos, animal shelters, aquariums, botanical gardens, or museums in your area.
- Talk to an agricultural scientist about his or her career.

Plant breeders apply genetics and biotechnology to improve plants' yield, quality, and the ability to withstand harsh weather, disease, and insects.

Plant pathologists research plant diseases and the decay of plant products to identify symptoms, determine causes, and develop control measures.

Soil scientists study the physical, chemical, and biological characteristics of soils to determine the most productive and effective planting strategies. Their research helps produce larger, healthier crops and farming procedures that are easier on the environment.

Words to Learn

agronomy the science of soil management and the production of field crops

biosecurity protecting agricultural resources from anything that might hurt plant and animal crops; this might include diseases, other animals and plants, terrorism, and anything else that may affect crop yield and food safety

biotechnology the use of live organisms (plant and animal cells) to manufacture new products

crop rotation the system of alternating crops planted in the same ground to protect the quality of the soil

crop yield the amount of a crop that is harvested at the end of a growing season

erosion the wearing away of soil and other land features by water, wind, and human activities, such as farming and construction

genes the units of heredity that are passed from parents to offspring

and control traits such as hair color and height among others

genetics the study of inheritance, or how living things resemble or differ from their ancestors

industrial crops crops used for industrial purposes rather than for human or animal food

livestock cattle, sheep, and other animals raised on a farm

nanotechnology the study of materials at the nanometer range—one-billionth of a meter

organic farming producing crops without chemicals

sustainable agriculture a type of agriculture that seeks to produce crops while protecting the environment and preserving the health of farmland for future generations

topsoil the surface soil that includes the layer where most plants have their roots

Those who specialize in improving the way animals are housed, bred, and fed are called *animal scientists.* They try to control diseases that farm animals and pets get. Some study only one kind of animal, such as dairy cattle; these scientists might study how cows' eating habits affect their milk supply. Others may study only poultry (chickens, turkeys, and ducks) in order to improve the quality and quantity of their eggs and their overall health.

Food scientists use their backgrounds in chemistry, microbiology, and other sciences to develop new or better ways of preserving, packaging, processing, storing, and delivering foods.

Agricultural engineers are specialized engineers who work in the food and agriculture industries. They help make farming easier and more profitable through the introduction of new farm machinery and through advancements in soil and water conservation.

To be a successful agricultural scientist, you should like conducting research and solving problems. You should be curious about the natural world. You should work well both alone and with a team of scientists and assistants. The ability to concentrate for long periods of time in front of a microscope or while conducting other types of research is also important. If you conduct research in the field, you should be in good physical shape. Field research involves a lot of walking, climbing, and bending and stooping to collect samples.

Education and Training

If you like science and are interested in animals and plants, a career in agricultural science may be for you. When you get to high school, you will have to take courses in English, mathe-matics, government, and history, as well as biology, chemistry, physics, and any other available science courses. You must also learn basic computer skills, including programming.

After high school, you will have to go to college to earn a bachelor's degree, which may be enough for some beginning jobs. A Ph.D. is usually required for teaching in a college or uni-versity, or for directing a research program. Many colleges and universities offer agricultural science programs. While earning an advanced degree, you will work on research projects, and you will write a research paper, called a dissertation, on your special area of study. You will also do fieldwork and laboratory research along with your classroom studies.

Earnings

According to the U.S. Department of Labor, the median annu-al salary of soil and plant scientists was approximately $58,390 in 2008. Salaries ranged from less than 34,260 to $105,340 or more per year.

Outlook

Employment for agricultural scientists will be good. The fields of biotechnology, nanotechnology, biosecurity, genetics, and sustainable agriculture will hold the best opportunities for ag-ricultural scientists. Employment growth for animal scientists should be slightly less strong than that of soil and plant scien-tists and food scientists and technologists.

Agricultural scientists with doctorates will have the most opportunities. Those with bachelor's and master's degrees will find plenty of work as technicians or in farm management.

FOR MORE INFO

To learn about opportunities for scientists in the dairy industry, visit the association's Web site.
American Dairy Science Association
http://www.adsa.org

To learn more about careers, contact
American Society of Agricultural and Biological Engineers
2950 Niles Road
St. Joseph, MI 49085-8607
269-429-0300
hq@asabe.org
http://www.asae.org

For information on careers, contact
American Society of Agronomy
5585 Guilford Road
Madison, WI 53711-5801
608-273-8080
http://www.agronomy.org

For career information, including articles and books, contact
Biotechnology Industry Organization
1201 Maryland Avenue, SW, Suite 900
Washington, DC 20024-2149
202-962-9200
info@bio.org
http://www.bio.org

For information on careers, contact
Crop Science Society of America
5585 Guilford Road
Madison, WI 53711-5801
http://www.crops.org

For information on accredited food science programs, visit the IFT Web site.
Institute of Food Technologists (IFT)
525 West Van Buren, Suite 1000
Chicago, IL 60607-3830
800-438-3663
info@ift.org
http://www.ift.org

For more information on agricultural careers and student programs, contact
National FFA Organization
6060 FFA Drive
PO Box 68960
Indianapolis, IN 46268-0960
317-802-6060
http://www.ffa.org

For general information about bioenergy, contact
Renewable Fuels Association
One Massachusetts Avenue, NW, Suite 820
Washington, DC 20001-1401
202-289-3835
http://www.ethanolrfa.org

To read *Soils Sustain Life*, visit the society's Web site.
Soil Science Society of America
5585 Guilford Road
Madison, WI 53711-5801
608-273-8080
http://www.soils.org

Visit the USDA Web site for more information on its agencies and programs as well as news releases.
U.S. Department of Agriculture (USDA)
1400 Independence Avenue, SW
Washington, DC 20250-0002
202-720-2791
http://www.usda.gov

Astronomers

What Astronomers Do

Astronomers study the universe and all the celestial, or cosmic, bodies in space. They use telescopes, computers, and complex measuring tools to find the positions of stars and planets. They calculate the orbits of comets, asteroids, and artificial satellites. They study how celestial objects form and deteriorate. They try to figure out how the universe started.

With special equipment, astronomers collect and analyze information about planets and stars, such as temperature, shape, size, brightness, and motion. They try to explain how the universe came to exist, how elements formed, why galaxies look the way they do, and whether there is other life in the universe.

Because the field of astronomy is so broad, astronomers usually focus on one area of study. For example, *stellar astronomers* study the stars. *Solar astronomers* study the Sun. *Planetary astronomers* study conditions on the planets. *Cosmologists* study the origin and the structure of the universe, and *astrophysicists* study the physical and chemical changes that happen in the universe. *Celestial mechanics specialists* study the motion and position of planets and other objects in the solar system. *Radio astronomers* study the source and nature of celestial radio waves using sensitive radio telescopes.

Most astronomers teach at universities or colleges. A few lecture at planetariums and teach classes for the public. Some work at research institutions or at observatories. Those who work at observatories spend three to six nights a month observing the night sky through a telescope. They spend the rest of

EXPLORING

- Read books about astronomy. Here are a few suggestions: *Astronomy: Out of This World!*, by Dan Green (Kingfisher, 2009); *The Manga Guide to the Universe*, by Ishikawa Kenji (No Starch Press, 2010); and *George's Secret Key to the Universe* and *George's Cosmic Treasure Hunt*, both by Stephen and Lucy Hawking (Simon & Schuster Children's Publishing, 2009).

- There are many astronomy sites on the Internet. The National Aeronautics and Space Administration (NASA) has a Web site especially for kids. You can learn about Earth and the other planets, space travel, the stars and galaxies, and NASA. You can even watch exciting videos of astronauts and spaceships. Here's the address: http://www. nasa.gov/audience/forkids/ home. Here are a few more Web site suggestions: *A New Universe to Discover: Careers in Astronomy* (http://aas.org/ education/careers.php), Intro to Astronomy (http://www. astronomy.com/asy/default. aspx?c=ps&id=6), Ask the Space Scientist (http://image. gsfc.nasa.gov/poetry/ask/ask-mag.html), Astronomy Today (http://www.astronomytoday. com), Rader's COSMOS4KIDS! (http://www.cosmos4kids. com), and Spaceweather.com (http://www.spaceweather. com).

- Join an amateur astronomy club. There are many such clubs all over the country. These clubs usually have telescopes and will let members of the public view the night skies.

- Visit a nearby planetarium and ask astronomers who work there about their jobs. Planetariums also help you learn more about the universe and see if this is a career you would like.

- Ask a counselor or teacher to help arrange an informational interview with an astronomer.

DID YOU KNOW?

- There are eight planets in our solar system. They orbit the Sun. The closest planet to the Sun is Mercury, followed by Venus, Mars, Earth, Jupiter, Saturn, Uranus, and Neptune.
- The Earth is about 93 million miles away from the Sun.
- Our Sun is so large that you could fit one million Earths inside.
- The Moon is just one-quarter the size of the Earth.

- The Moon has a wide range of temperature extremes. In the daytime, its mean temperature is 225°F. At night, its mean temperature is −243°F.
- Asteroids can be as tiny as a pebble. The largest known asteroid is Ceres. It is about 580 miles in diameter.

Source: Astronomy.com

their time in offices or laboratories where they study, analyze their data, and write reports. Other astronomers work for government agencies or private industry.

Education and Training

You can begin training to become an astronomer in high school. You should plan to take classes in math, chemistry, physics, geography, and foreign languages (especially French, German, and Russian). Because astronomy is a high-technology field, you should try to learn as much as you can about computers.

After high school, you will have to earn a bachelor's degree in physics, mathematics, or astronomy. Once you receive your bachelor's degree, you may find work as an assistant or researcher. Most astronomers go on to earn both a master's degree and a doctorate.

Earnings

Astronomers had average earnings of $101,300 in 2008, according to the U.S. Department of Labor. Salaries ranged from less than $45,000 to $156,000 or more annually. The average

Tips for Success

To be a successful astronomer, you should

- have a good imagination
- enjoy solving problems
- be an excellent researcher
- have strong communication skills
- enjoy traveling
- have good mathematical skills
- be willing to continue to learn throughout your career

for astronomers employed by the federal government was $125,000. Those who worked for colleges and universities earned about $79,000.

Outlook

Astronomy is one of the smallest science fields, so people trained in astronomy must compete with many others for the best jobs. Many astronomers find jobs in universities and government agencies. Job opportunities are expected to be good in these settings. Astronomy graduates with just a bachelor's degree will find it hard to get top research positions. Instead, they can find work as high school science teachers or work as science technicians in private industry.

FOR MORE INFO

Visit the FAQ section at the following Web site to read the article "Career Profile: Astronomy."
American Association of Amateur Astronomers
PO Box 7981
Dallas, TX 75209-0981
aaaa@astromax.com
http://www.astromax.com

To read "A New Universe to Discover: A Guide to Careers in Astronomy," visit the society's Web site.
American Astronomical Society
2000 Florida Avenue, NW, Suite 400

Washington, DC 20009-1231
202-328-2010
aas@aas.org
http://www.aas.org

This organization is a resource for professionals who work in many physics disciplines, including astronomy. For more information, contact
American Institute of Physics
One Physics Ellipse
College Park, MD 20740-3843
301-209-3100
aipinfo@aip.org
http://www.aip.org

Biologists

What Biologists Do

Biologists are scientists who study how plants and animals grow and reproduce. They are sometimes called *biological scientists* or *life scientists.* Biologists often have other job titles because they specialize in one area of biology. *Botanists,* for example, study different types of plants. *Wildlife biologists* study the habitats and the conditions necessary for the survival of birds and other wildlife. *Zoologists* study different types of animals. They are usually identified by the animals they study: *ichthyologists* (fish), *mammalogists* (mammals), *ornithologists* (birds), and *herpetologists* (reptiles and amphibians).

Biologists conduct research in the field or in the laboratory. Their exact job duties vary depending on their area of interest. For example, *aquatic biologists* study plants and animals that live in water. They may do much of their research on a boat. They study the water temperature, amount of light, salt levels, and other environmental conditions in the oceans, streams, rivers, or lakes. They then observe how

EXPLORING

- Visit Web sites to learn more about biology. Here is one suggestion: Rader's BIOLOGY4KIDS! (http://www.biology4kids.com).
- You can learn about the work of biologists by taking school field trips to nature centers, laboratories, parks, and research centers.
- Visit local museums of natural history or science, aquariums, and zoos.
- Many park districts offer classes and field trips to help you explore plant and animal life. Take part in these activities to learn more about the field.
- Talk to a biologist about his or her career.

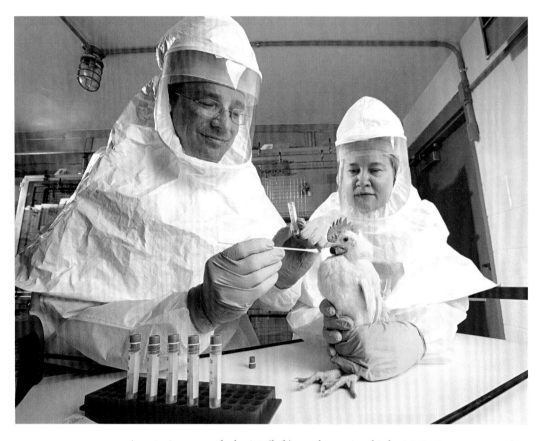

A veterinary pathologist (left) *and a microbiologist test a new vaccine.* (Stephen Ausmus, USDA, Agricultural Research Service)

fish and other plants and animals react to these environments. *Marine biologists* are specialized aquatic biologists who focus on plants and animals that live in oceans. *Entomologists* study insects and their relationship to other life forms. *Limnologists* study freshwater organisms and their environment. *Mycologists* study edible, poisonous, and parasitic fungi, such as mushrooms, molds, yeasts, and mildews, to determine which are useful to medicine, agriculture, and industry. *Biochemists* study the chemical makeup of living organisms. *Biophysicists* apply physical principles to biological problems. *Microbiologists* study bacteria, viruses, molds, algae, yeasts, and other organisms of microscopic or submicroscopic size. *Molecular biologists* apply their research to animal and bacterial systems to help improve and better understand human health.

Some biologists even help police solve crimes. *Forensic biologists* use scientific principles and methods to study biological specimens so they can be used as evidence in a court of law.

No matter what type of research biologists do, they must keep careful records to note all procedures and results. Because biologists may sometimes work with dangerous chemicals and other materials, they always must take safety precautions and carefully follow each step in an experiment.

Activities for Budding Biologists

If you have one of these hobbies, you may have a future as a biologist:

- Birdwatching
- Collecting butterflies and other insects
- Gardening
- Microscope study
- Raising or caring for animals
- Watching nature shows
- Visiting nature preserves
- Going to the zoo

Some biologists give advice to businesses. Many biologists work for government agencies at the local, state, and federal levels. Some examples of federal employers of biologists include the U.S. Department of the Interior, the U.S. Fish and Wildlife Service, the U.S. Public Health Service, and the National Oceanic and Atmospheric Administration. Others inspect foods and other products. Many biologists write articles for scientific journals. Some may also teach at schools or universities.

Biologists need to be good researchers and problem solvers. They should also have patience because they often spend much time in observation in laboratories and in the field. Biologists must also have good communication skills in order to work well with others and explain their findings orally and in writing.

DID YOU KNOW?

- There are approximately 1.8 million species of animals, plants, and other living things on Earth.
- There are five kingdoms of life on Earth: monera (single-celled organisms that do not have a nucleus, or a control center; bacteria are the only type of monera); protists (single-celled organisms that have a nucleus—examples include algae and amoeba); fungi (examples include mushrooms and molds); plants; and animals.
- There are about 260,000 plant species on Earth.

Education and Training

If you are thinking about a career in biology, you should plan to take high school courses in biology, chemistry, mathematics, physics, and a foreign language.

After high school you must go to college, where you will take more advanced courses in biology, math, chemistry, and physics. Then you choose a specialty. Specialties include microbiology, bacteriology, botany, ecology, or anatomy. Most successful biologists also have a master's degree or a doctorate in biology or a related field.

Biologists who have advanced degrees will have the best chances of obtaining challenging and good-paying jobs. Those with only a bachelor's degree will find work as science or engineering technicians, health technologists and technicians, and high school biology teachers.

Earnings

Salaries for biologists ranged from $35,000 to more than $101,000 a year in 2008, according to the U.S. Department of Labor. The average salary was $65,000. Government biologists with bachelor's degrees earned salaries of about $70,270 a year. Microbiologists earned median salaries of $64,000; zoologists and wildlife biologists, $55,000; and college biology professors, $71,000.

Outlook

Employment for biologists should be very good in the future. Biologists will continue to be needed to help solve environ-

FOR MORE INFO

For information about a career as a biologist, contact
American Institute of Biological Sciences
1444 I Street, NW, Suite 200
Washington, DC 20005-6535
202-628-1500
http://www.aibs.org

For information on educational programs, contact
American Society for Biochemistry and Molecular Biology
9650 Rockville Pike
Bethesda, MD 20814-3996
301-634-7145
http://www.asbmb.org

For information on careers, contact
American Society for Cell Biology
8120 Woodmont Avenue, Suite 750
Bethesda, MD 20814-2762
301-347-9300
http://www.ascb.org

For career information for middle and high school students, visit the society's Web site.
American Society for Microbiology
1752 N Street, NW
Washington, DC 20036-2904

202-737-3600
http://www.asm.org

For career information, including articles and books, contact
Biotechnology Industry Organization
1201 Maryland Avenue, SW, Suite 900
Washington, DC 20024-2149
202-962-9200
info@bio.org
http://www.bio.org

For information on botany careers, contact
Botanical Society of America
PO Box 299
St. Louis, MO 63166-0299
314-577-9566
bsa-manager@botany.org
http://www.botany.org

For information about careers, contact
Society for Integrative and Comparative Biology
1313 Dolley Madison Boulevard, Suite 402
McLean, VA 22101-3926
800-955-1236
http://www.sicb.org

mental problems. Opportunities will be best for biochemists and biophysicists. Only a small number of people work in many biology specialties, so there will always be competition for good jobs.

Botanists

What Botanists Do

Botanists are scientists who study plants. They study cell structure and how plants reproduce. They also study how plants are distributed on Earth; how rainfall, climate, and other conditions affect them; and more.

Botany is a major branch of biology. Botanists play an important part in modern science and industry. Their work affects agriculture, agronomy, conservation, forestry, and horticulture. Botanists develop new drugs to treat diseases. They find food resources for people in poor countries. They discover solutions to environmental problems.

Botanists who specialize in agriculture or agronomy try to develop new varieties of crops that better resist disease. Or they may try to improve the growth of crops such as high-yield corn. These botanists focus on a specific type of plant species, such as ferns (pteridology), or plants that are native to a specific area, such as wetland or desert. Some botanists work in private industry at food or drug companies. They may develop new products or they may test and inspect products.

Research botanists work at research stations operated by colleges and universities and botanical gardens. Botanists who work in conservation or ecology often do their work out in the field. They help recreate lost or damaged ecosystems, direct pollution cleanups, and take inventories of species.

There are many different types of botanists. *Ethnobotanists* study how plants are used by a particular culture or ethnic

EXPLORING

- Visit the following Web sites to view photos of plants: Kid-ScienceLink.com (http://www.kidsciencelink.com/botany) and Botanical Society of America (http://www.botany.org/plantimages).
- The Botanical Society of America offers a membership category for amateur botanists. Contact the society for more information.
- Take part in science fairs and clubs.
- Volunteer to work for parks, nurseries, farms, labs, camps, florists, or landscape architects.
- Tour a botanical garden in your area and talk to staff.
- Grow your own garden, including fruits and vegetables, herbs, flowers, and indoor plants. Keep a notebook to record how each plant responds to watering, fertilizing, and sunlight.
- Take camping trips or hike to learn more about the natural world.

group to treat diseases and injuries. *Ecologists* study the connection between plants and animals and the physical environment. They restore native species to areas, repair damaged ecosystems, and work on pollution problems. *Forest ecologists* focus on forest species and their habitats, such as forest wetlands. *Mycologists* study fungi and apply their findings to medicine, agriculture, and industry. Mushrooms and yeast are examples of fungi. *Plant cytologists* use powerful microscopes to study plant tissues in order to discover why some cells become malignant (unhealthy) and cause the plant to get sick or die. *Plant geneticists* study the origin and development of inherited traits (or qualities), such as size and color.

DID YOU KNOW?

Facts About Fungi

- Mushrooms, toadstools, and molds are types of fungi.
- Fungi can live anywhere, but like damp, shady areas the best.
- Fungi help break down dead plants and animals and turn them into soil.
- Some mushrooms taste good and are safe to eat.
- Other mushrooms, such as Death Cap and Destroying Angel, are deadly to eat. Never eat a mushroom you find in a field, a forest, or in your yard!
- Yeast, a type of fungus, is used to brew beer and make bread.
- Penicillin is produced by a fungus. It is used by doctors to fight bacterial infections in people and animals.

Source: NatureGrid.org.uk

There are other types of botanists. *Morphologists* study macroscopic plant forms and life cycles (those that can be viewed by the human eye). *Palyologists* study pollen and spores. *Pteridologists* study ferns and other related plants. *Bryologists* study mosses and similar plants. *Lichenologists* study lichens, which are dual organisms made of both alga and fungus. *Forensic botanists* collect and analyze plant material found at crime scenes.

Botanists have a deep love for plants and nature and also enjoy science. They should be very organized, curious, and able to work well alone or with other people. They should also have good communication skills.

Education and Training

In high school, take as many biology and earth science classes as possible. You should also take college prep courses in chemistry, physics, mathematics, English, and foreign language.

If you want to become a botanist, you will have to go to college and earn a bachelor's degree. People who want to work in research and teaching positions have to study even longer. They go on to earn a master's or even a doctoral degree. These higher degrees require you to specialize in one of the many areas of botany mentioned in the section What Botanists Do. For example, a master's degree in conservation biology focuses on the conservation of specific plant and animal communities.

Earnings

The National Association of Colleges and Employers reports that those with a bachelor's degree in biological and life sciences earned average starting salaries of $33,254 in July 2009. Most botanists earned between $48,000 and $73,000 in 2010, according to Salary.com. The most experienced botanists earned more than $85,000 a year.

Outlook

Employment for botanists is expected to be good. Botanists will be needed to help with environmental, conservation, and pharmaceutical issues. Botanists work in such a wide variety of fields that they are almost guaranteed to have a job.

It's a Bug's Life

Though many bugs are harmful to plants, some can be beneficial. These bugs prey on plant-feeding insects, and it isn't pretty!

- Ladybugs eat aphids, mealy bugs, and mites. Adults may eat 50 or more aphids a day.
- Praying mantis kill their plant-feeding prey by biting the back of the neck, severing the main nerves.
- Lacewings suck the body fluids from their prey and carry the remains of their victims on their backs.
- Hover flies grasp plant-feeding insects and puncture them using tiny hooks in their mouths.

FOR MORE INFO

For information about a career as a biologist, contact
American Institute of Biological Sciences
1444 I Street, NW, Suite 200
Washington, DC 20005-6535
202-628-1500
http://www.aibs.org

For general information about plant biology, contact
American Society of Plant Biologists
http://www.aspb.org

For career information, including articles and books, contact
Biotechnology Industry Organization
1201 Maryland Avenue, SW, Suite 900
Washington, DC 20024-2149
202-962-9200
info@bio.org
http://www.bio.org

Visit the society's Web site for information on careers in botany.
Botanical Society of America
PO Box 299
St. Louis, MO 63166-0299

314-577-9566
http://www.botany.org

Contact this organization for information on volunteer positions in natural resource management for high school students.
Student Conservation Association
689 River Road
PO Box 550
Charlestown, NH 03603-0550
603-543-1700
ask-us@thesca.org
http://www.thesca.org

This government agency manages more than 535 national wildlife refuges. The service's Web site has information on volunteer opportunities, careers, and answers to frequently asked questions.
U.S. Fish & Wildlife Service
U.S. Department of the Interior
1849 C Street, NW
Washington, DC 20240-0001
800-344-WILD
contact@fws.gov
http://www.fws.gov

Employment for botanists who work for the government may not be as strong. When the economy is weak, government agencies may have less funding to hire botanists. When the economy is strong, there will be more money to hire botanists to conduct research.

Botanists with advanced degrees and years of experience in the field will have the best job prospects.

Chemists

What Chemists Do

Chemistry is the study of the physical and chemical properties of matter (solids, liquids, and gases). *Chemists* are scientists who improve products and create new ones, such as drugs, synthetic plastics, and fabrics. They also improve rocket fuels for space travel, and they develop processes for obtaining light metals such as aluminum, magnesium, and titanium. Chemists work in many fields. The following paragraphs detail some of the many types of chemists.

Food chemists develop new foods and ways to make them stay fresh longer. They study how methods of cooking, canning, freezing, and packaging affect the taste, appearance, and quality of different food products. Food chemists test samples of meats, cereals, and dairy products to make sure that they meet government food standards.

Analytical chemists study the composition of substances, or what substances are made of, and analyze them. They set standards for safe levels of chemicals in drinking water. They check for pollutants in wastewater from industrial plants.

Biochemists, also known as *biological chemists,* study the composition and actions of complex chemicals in living organisms. They identify and analyze the chemical processes related to biological functions, such as metabolism or reproduction. They also conduct genetic studies and work in the pharmaceutical and food industries.

The distinction between organic and inorganic chemistry is based on carbon-hydrogen compounds. Ninety-nine

EXPLORING

- Visit Web sites about chemistry and careers in the field. Here are two suggestions: Rader's CHEM4KIDS! (http://www.chem4kids.com) and Women in Chemistry (http://www.chemheritage.org/women_chemistry).
- Ask your teacher to help you with chemistry experiments.
- There are junior chemistry sets available that teach you about the scientific method, how to perform chemical experiments, and chemical words and phrases.

- Your school or community librarian can help you find chemistry books and computer programs.
- Contact the department of chemistry at a local college or university to discuss the field and arrange tours of its laboratories or classrooms.
- Once you get into high school, you can compete in the Chemistry Olympiad. Visit http://www.chemistry.org for more information.
- Talk to a chemist about his or her career.

percent of all chemicals that occur naturally contain carbon. *Organic chemists* study the chemical compounds that contain carbon and hydrogen, while *inorganic chemists* study all other substances.

Physical chemists study the physical characteristics of atoms (the smallest units of matter) and molecules (a group of at least two atoms).

Toxicologists study the by-products, or side effects, that are produced by paint, petroleum, leather, and pharmaceutical manufacturing, among other things. They design ways to prevent harmful effects on users of the products and on the environment.

To be a successful chemist, you should have a detail-oriented personality since you will often work with very small quantities and take minute (tiny) measurements. You should be curious and enjoy solving problems. You should be able to work well both alone and in a team of other chemists and technicians. Strong communication skills will help you work well with others and write reports and articles about your findings.

Education and Training

Training for a career in chemistry begins in high school. You should take at least three or four years of mathematics, including algebra, geometry, and calculus; three years of science,

A chemist works on the final steps of turning algae into a fuel source. (Marcio Jose Sanchez, AP Photo)

including biology, chemistry, and physics; and four years of English. Computer classes are also important.

After high school, you must go to college to earn a bachelor's degree, which will qualify you for an entry-level job. Higher-level jobs require more education. To become a researcher in industry, a master's or a doctoral degree is necessary. Almost all college and university research and teaching positions require a doctoral degree.

Profile: Dorothy Crowfoot Hodgkin (1910–1994)

Dorothy Crowfoot Hodgkin was a groundbreaking chemist who helped confirm the molecular structure of penicillin, an antibiotic that has helped saved countless lives around the world. She is also known for her work studying cholesterol, vitamin B_{12}, and insulin.

Hodgkin was born in Cairo, Egypt, to English parents. She grew up in the Middle East and in England. From a young age, she was interested in science—especially the study of crystals. She attended the University of Oxford, where she studied chemistry and physics. She also undertook a research project in which she studied X-ray crystallography. The process is complicated, but it basically involves turning a substance into a crystal (if it is not already crystal-lized) and shooting X-rays at it to determine its structure. Hodgkin also studied at the University of Cambridge.

In 1945, Hodgkin, working with other scientists, was finally able to determine the molecular structure of penicillin. This allowed it to be more easily and less expensively mass-produced in laboratories.

In 1964, Hodgkin won the Nobel Prize in Chemistry "for her determinations by X-ray techniques of the structures of important biochemical substances." She worked as a researcher and teacher at Somerville College until her retirement in 1977.

Source: Women in Chemistry

Earnings

Chemists' salaries depend on ability, education, experience, the nature of the job, and where you work. The National Association of Colleges and Employers reports that those with a bachelor's degree in chemistry earned average starting salaries of $39,897 in July 2009. Most chemists earned between $48,000 and $90,000 in 2008, according to the U.S. Department of Labor. An experienced chemist with a Ph.D. and supervisory duties can earn $113,000 a year or more.

DID YOU KNOW?

Where Chemists Work

- Chemical manufacturing companies
- Food manufacturing companies
- Federal government (such as the Departments of Health and Human Services, Agriculture, and Energy)
- State and local government agencies
- Colleges and universities

Outlook

Employment opportunities for chemists will only be fair during the next decade. Most openings will be in biotechnology, pharmaceuticals, and firms that produce specialty chemicals. Job opportunities are expected to decrease for chemists in industrial chemical and petroleum industries. Because competition is so strong, you will need a doctoral degree to be qualified for the best jobs. Those with just a bachelor's degree can work as high school chemistry teachers or chemical technicians and technologists.

FOR MORE INFO

Visit the association's Web site for information on publications and to read industry news.

American Association for Clinical Chemistry
1850 K Street, NW, Suite 625
Washington, DC 20006-2215
800-892-1400
http://www.aacc.org

For general information about chemistry careers and education programs, contact
American Chemical Society
1155 16th Street, NW
Washington, DC 20036-4839
800-227-5558
http://www.chemistry.org

For information about chemicals and the chemical industry, contact
American Chemistry Council
1300 Wilson Boulevard
Arlington, VA 22209-2323

703-741-5000
http://www.americanchemistry.com

For career information, including articles and books, contact
Biotechnology Industry Organization
1201 Maryland Avenue, SW, Suite 900
Washington, DC 20024-2149
202-962-9200
info@bio.org
http://www.bio.org

For information on careers in the cosmetics industry, contact
Society of Cosmetic Chemists
120 Wall Street, Suite 2400
New York, NY 10005-4088
212-668-1500
SCC@SCConline.org
http://www.scconline.org

Ecologists

What Ecologists Do

Ecologists are specialized scientists. They study how plants and animals interact with and sustain each other in their environments, or habitat. An environment includes living things, but it also includes nonliving elements, such as chemicals, moisture, soil, light, temperature, and things made by humans, such as buildings, highways, machines, fertilizers, and medicines. The word *ecology* is sometimes used to describe the balance of nature.

A big part of an ecologist's job is to study communities. A community is a group of organisms that share a particular habitat. For example, *forest ecologists* might study how changes in the environment affect forests. They may study what causes a certain type of tree to grow well, including light and soil requirements, and resistance to insects and disease.

Some ecologists study biomes, which are large communities. Examples of biomes are the tropical rain forest, the prairie, the tundra, and the desert. The ocean is sometimes considered as one biome.

Many ecologists study ecosystems—a living community together with its nonliving components. *Population ecologists* study why a certain population of living things increases, decreases, or remains stable.

Restoration ecologists create and implement plans to reestablish ecosystems that have been damaged by humans or natural events such as flooding.

EXPLORING

- Read books and other publications about ecology and the environment. You will find lots of reading material at your library or bookstore and on the Internet.
- Join a school ecology club.
- Learn more about environmental issues such as global warming, deforestation, pollution, and endangered species by contacting environmental organizations and reading newspapers.
- Join a scouting organization or environmental protection group to gain firsthand experience in the work of an ecologist.
- Visit natural history museums to learn more about the field.

- Visit nearby parks or forest preserves. What kinds of trees and plants grow there? Which insects, animals, and birds are native to the area?
- Learn about what type of environmental problems (such as pollution) are affecting your town or city.
- Talk to an ecologist about his or her career. Ask the following questions: What made you want to become an ecologist? What do you like most and least about your job? How did you train to become an ecologist? What advice would you give to someone who is interested in the career?

All living things, including humans, depend on their environments to live. As a result, the work of ecologists is extremely important in helping us understand how environments work. An example of how the study of ecology helps us is farming. Ecologists help farmers grow crops in the right soils and climates, provide livestock with suitable food and shelter, and get rid of harmful pests, such as insects or other animals that eat or damage crops. The study of ecology helps protect, improve,

An ecologist measures plant and flower heads while a technician uses a sweep net to gather samples. (Peggy Greb, USDA, Agricultural Research Service)

and preserve our environment. Ecologists study industry and government actions and help fix past environmental problems.

Most ecologists work in land and water conservation jobs in the public sector. This includes the federal government, the largest employer. The Bureau of Land Management, the U.S. Fish and Wildlife Service, the National Park Service, and the U.S. Geological Survey are among the federal agencies that employ ecologists. Other public sector opportunities are with regional, state, and local agencies. Opportunities in the private sector can be found with utilities, timber companies, and consulting firms. Some ecologists work as teachers at nature centers, middle schools and high schools, and colleges and universities.

Ecological Catastrophe

Humans sometimes try to improve the environment and end up making big mistakes because they don't understand ecological balance. Ecological balance can be defined as the way in which plants and animals live together. An example of an ecological catastrophe, or disaster, occurred on Borneo (a large island in Southeast Asia) shortly after World War II (1939–1945). A program was started there to control mosquitoes by spraying DDT, an insecticide that can hurt humans and other animals if swallowed or absorbed through the skin. The number of mosquitoes declined drastically, but the roofs of houses began to collapse because they were being eaten by caterpillars. The caterpillars had previously been held under control by certain predatory wasps—which had been killed off by the DDT.

In addition to spraying for mosquitoes, the villagers also sprayed inside their homes to kill flies. Previously, the houseflies had been more or less controlled by lizards called geckos. As the geckos continued eating houseflies, now laden with DDT, the geckos began to die. The dead or dying geckos were eaten by house cats. The cats also began to die from the DDT concentrated in the bodies of the geckos they were eating. So many cats died that rats began invading the houses, eating the villagers' food. The number of rats grew quickly and eventually became potential carriers of plague (a deadly disease). This example shows how careful we need to be when trying to fix an environmental problem. We have to think about what can go wrong or right during every move we make. Otherwise, disaster can happen.

Words to Learn

canopy the upper layer of a forest, created by the foliage and branches of the tallest trees

coniferous trees that bear cones (which contain seeds)

ecosystem a community of animals and plants and their interaction with the nonliving environment

effluent wastewater or sewage that flows into a river, lake, or ocean

erosion the wearing away of soil and other land features by water, wind, and human activities, such as farming and construction

deforestation when all the trees in a particular area are cut down or burned; deforestation causes great harm to the plants, humans, and other animals that live in the affected area

fertilizer natural and chemical elements that help plants to grow; chemical fertilizers can be harmful if overused

global warming the slow rise in the Earth's average temperature caused by an increase in greenhouse gases (such as carbon dioxide, methane, and nitrous oxide); many people believe global warming is having a negative effect on the environment

habitat an area where an organism or group of organisms normally lives

riparian zone forest or grass growing on the banks of a stream; the riparian zone can prevent soil erosion

savanna a flat, grassy plain found in tropical areas

tundra a cold region where the soil under the surface of the ground is permanently frozen

watershed the gathering ground of a river system, a ridge that separates two river basins, or an area of land that slopes into a river or lake

Education and Training

Classes that will be useful include earth science, biology, ecology, chemistry, English, and math. Ecologists often use computers to do research and record their findings. For that reason, you should also take computer science courses.

To be an ecologist you must go to college and earn a bachelor of science degree. Recommended majors are biology, botany, chemistry, ecology, geology, physics, or zoology.

You will need a master's degree for research or management jobs. If you want to work as a college teacher or research supervisor, you will need a doctoral degree.

Earnings

Salaries for ecologists vary depending on such factors as their level of education, experience, area of specialization, and the organization for which they work. Ecologists just starting out in the field might make $36,000 or less. Those with many years in the field earn $63,000 or more.

Outlook

The job outlook for environmental workers in general should remain good during the next decade. Opportunities should be best for ecologists who work for environmental consulting firms in the private sector. There will be fewer jobs in land and water conservation. This is because so many ecologists compete for these popular jobs. Also, many environmental organizations don't have a large amount of money available to hire ecologists.

Ecologists with advanced degrees who are willing to travel to different parts of the United States and the world will have the best job opportunities.

FOR MORE INFO

For a wide variety of publications, including *Issues in Ecology, Careers in Ecology,* and fact sheets about specific ecological concerns, contact
Ecological Society of America
1990 M Street, NW, Suite 700
Washington, DC 20036-3415
202-833-8773
esahq@esa.org
http://esa.org

For information about internships and volunteer opportunities for teens, contact
National Wildlife Federation
11100 Wildlife Center Drive
Reston, VA 20190-5362

800-822-9919
http://www.nwf.org

Contact this organization for information on volunteer positions in natural resource management for high school students.
Student Conservation Association
689 River Road
PO Box 550
Charlestown, NH 03603-0550
603-543-1700
ask-us@thesca.org
http://www.thesca.org

Forensic Experts

What Forensic Experts Do

The American Academy of Forensic Sciences defines forensic science as any science that is "used in public, in a court, or in the justice system." *Forensic experts* collect and examine evidence of crimes. They use a variety of equipment to analyze body fluids, fibers, fabric, dust, soils, paint chips, glass fragments, fire accelerants, paper and ink, and other substances gathered at crime scenes and other locations. The equipment they use includes spectroscopes, microscopes, gas chromatographs, infrared and ultraviolet light, and microphotography. They analyze poisons, drugs, and other substances found in bodies by examining tissue samples, stomach contents, and blood samples. They analyze and classify blood, blood alcohol, semen, hair, fingernails, teeth, bones and tissue, and other biological specimens. Using samples of the genetic material DNA, they can match a person with a sample of body tissue. They study documents to find out whether they are forged (fake) or genuine. They also examine the physical properties of firearms, bullets, and explosives.

Some forensic experts travel to crime scenes. They collect and label evidence. They search for bullet casings, blood drips, or bits of an exploded bomb and other objects scattered by an explosion. They look for footprints, fingerprints, and tire tracks, which must be recorded or preserved by plaster casting before they are wiped out. Forensic experts take notes and photographs to document the arrangement of objects, bodies, and debris. Some forensic experts work in crime laboratories

EXPLORING

- There are many books about forensic science and crime investigation in your school or local library. Here are a few suggestions: *Forensic Scientist: Careers Solving Crimes and Scientific Mysteries,* by Judith Williams (Enslow Publishers Inc., 2009); *Crime Scene: How Investigators Use Science to Track Down the Bad Guys,* 2nd edition, by Vivien Bowers (Maple Tree Press, 2006), *Forensic Science for High School Students,* by John Funkhouser (Kendall Hunt Publishing Company, 2005); and *Opportunities in Forensic Science Careers,* 2nd edition, by Blythe Camenson (McGraw-Hill, 2008).
- Participating in science clubs will help you become familiar with using microscopes and improve your observation skills.
- Ask your high school science teacher or career counselor to help arrange a tour of a crime lab or a presentation by a forensic expert.
- There are many interesting Web sites that provide more information about forensic science. For example, the American Academy of Forensic Sciences offers an overview of many forensic science careers at its Web site, http://www.aafs.org. Other interesting sites include CSI Web Adventures (http://forensics.rice.edu) and Learn About Forensics (http://www.drhenrylee.com/learn).
- Contact forensic science professional associations for more information about various specialties.

and rarely, if ever, travel to crime scenes. Many forensic experts testify in court about their findings.

The following paragraphs provide a brief overview of some of the most popular specialties in forensic science.

DID YOU KNOW?

Where Forensic Experts Work

- Large police departments
- State law enforcement agencies
- District attorneys' offices
- Medical examiners' offices
- Colleges and universities
- Insurance companies
- Self employment
- Federal government (including the FBI, the military, Drug Enforcement Administration, United States Postal Service, Secret Service, Central Intelligence Agency, U.S. Fish and Wildlife Service, and the Bureau of Alcohol, Tobacco, Firearms, and Explosives)

Computer forensics specialists are experts who examine computers and other technology for evidence of wrongdoing. They may also be known as *computer* or *cyber examiners.*

Fingerprint classifiers catalog and compare fingerprints of suspected criminals. They do this to find out if the people who left the fingerprints at the scene of a crime were involved in past crimes. They often try to match the fingerprints of unknown corpses (deceased people) with fingerprint records to establish their identity.

Fire investigators study the cause, origin, and circumstances of fires involving loss of life and considerable property damage. They interview witnesses and prepare investigation reports. They arrest and seek prosecution of arsonists. They are also known as *fire marshals.*

Forensic anthropologists examine and identify bones and skeletal remains for the purposes of homicide, scientific, archaeological, or judicial investigations.

Forensic biologists use scientific principles and methods to study biological specimens so they can be used as evidence in a court of law.

Forensic botanists collect and analyze plant material found at crime scenes.

Forensic chemists conduct tests on evidence from crime scenes. Evidence ranges from paint chips, fire debris, and glass fragments, to hair and other biological evidence.

Forensic engineers study materials, devices, structures, and products that do not work as they were designed to or that failed to work completely. They have backgrounds in many different engineering fields.

Forensic entomologists use insect-related evidence and their knowledge of insects to provide facts in civil and crimi-

Fame & Fortune: Dr. Henry Lee (1938–)

Dr. Henry Lee is one of the most famous forensic scientists in the world. During his career, which has spanned more than four decades, he has worked on more than 6,000 cases, including investigating war crimes in Bosnia and Croatia, the trial of O. J. Simpson, a review of the assassination of President John F. Kennedy, the investigation of the Washington, D.C., sniper attacks, and forensic investigations conducted after the 9/11 terrorist attacks. He has served as an expert witness in many court cases and is the coauthor of books such as *Cracking Cases: The Science of Solving Cases* and *Famous Crimes Revisited: From Sacco-Vanzetti to O.J. Simpson*. Dr. Lee once even solved a crime without the presence of a body!

Dr. Lee was born in China and grew up in Taiwan. As a young man, he worked as a police officer. Then in 1965 he decided to come to the United States to pursue his education. He was interested in forensic science, so he earned a bachelor's degree in the field from John Jay College. Then he went on to earn graduate degrees in biochemistry from New York University.

Dr. Lee founded the Forensic Science Program at the University of New Haven. In 2007, in appreciation of Dr. Lee's work, the university renamed its college of criminal justice the Henry C. Lee College of Criminal Justice and Forensic Sciences.

Dr. Lee has won many awards during his career, including the Distinguished Criminalist Award from the Academy of Forensic Sciences and the Donero Award from International Association of Identification. Today, he is the chief emeritus of the Connecticut State Police. He travels the world conducting seminars on forensic science—continuing to educate present and future forensic scientists about the field.

Dr. Lee says that hard work and the pursuit of excellence were the keys to his success. Visit http://www.drhenrylee.com for more information about Dr. Lee and his career.

Source: DrHenryLee.com

nal cases. They are sometimes called *medical entomologists* or *medicocriminal entomologists* in criminal investigations.

Forensic nurses are medical professionals who are trained to work with victims, suspects, and evidence of crimes.

Forensic odontologists are specially trained dentists who help identify human remains and compare bite marks to those of a particular person.

Forensic pathologists examine the deceased (usually those who die unexpectedly, suddenly, or violently) to determine cause and manner of death.

Forensic psychiatrists conduct psychiatric evaluations of accused criminals. They are often called to testify on whether the accused is mentally fit to stand trial.

Forensic toxicologists detect and identify the presence of poisons or drugs in a victim's body.

Questioned document examiners study a wide variety of documents to determine if they are authentic or if they have been altered in any manner. They are also known as *forensic document examiners* and *handwriting and typewriting identification experts*.

To be successful forensic expert, you should have a strong interest in science and solving mysteries. You should have a curious, but organized, personality. You should be able to make precise measurements and observations in laboratories and at crime scenes. Strong communication skills are important since you have to write reports about your findings, interact with coworkers, and sometimes testify in court. Other important traits are patience, persistence, honesty, and a good memory.

Education and Training

Courses in computers, mathematics, the physical sciences, photography, and English are good preparation for a career in forensic science. Most positions require at least a bachelor's degree. Advanced degrees are needed for top positions. Many colleges and universities offer programs in forensic science. A smaller number offer training in specialized forensic science fields. Some careers require a medical degree.

Earnings

Salaries for forensic experts vary by specialty, education level, location, and other factors. Earnings range from less than $35,000 to more than $100,000.

Outlook

Employment for forensic experts should be excellent during the next decade. Population increases, a rising crime rate, and the greater focus on scientific methodology in crime investigation will create demand for trained experts. It is important to remember that many forensic science fields are very small and employ only a small number of workers. That means that even if employment is strong in a field, it may still be difficult to find a job. Forensic experts with advanced education and a lot of experience will have the best job prospects.

Genetic Scientists

What Genetic Scientists Do

Genetic scientists, or *geneticists,* study heredity in plants and animals, including humans. Geneticists conduct research on how traits, or characteristics, are passed from one generation to the next through the genes present in each cell of an organism.

The goal of genetic scientists is to understand and cure genetic diseases, advise families who are at risk of having children with genetic disorders, and breed new crops and livestock. Most geneticists work in a laboratory. Besides having excellent mathematical and analytical skills, genetic scientists also must have good writing and teaching techniques. The following paragraphs detail specialties in the field.

Research geneticists try to identify genes that affect human behavior. Many work as professors at academic institutions or join the staffs of research institutes or biotechnology companies.

Genetic counselors work as a part of a health care team. They give information and support to families of children with birth disorders or genetic disorders. They also help people who have genetic conditions.

Clinical geneticists are doctors who study genetic disorders and birth disorders in patients, arrange for the proper treatment, and help the patients cope with the disorder.

Molecular geneticists study DNA, the blueprint for protein molecules in cells.

Forensic geneticists help the law enforcement community to perform DNA fingerprinting. Alec Jeffreys, a professor at Leices-

EXPLORING

- Read books about genetics. Here is one suggestion: *Genetics For Dummies,* by Tara Rodden Robinson (For Dummies, 2005). Although this book is geared for older students and adults, paging through it will give you a good general introduction to the field.
- Visit http://www.ashg.org/education/careers.shtml to learn more about careers in genetics.
- Visit http://learn.genetics.utah.edu/content/begin/ traits/tour_heredity.html to learn more about heredity.
- To prepare for a career in genetics, study science and math and experiment with a home chemistry kit.
- Ask your science teacher to contact departments of biology and genetics at nearby colleges and universities and arrange field trips or visits by speakers.
- Talk to a genetic scientist about his or her career.

ter University, discovered that each of us has highly specific patterns within our DNA. The pattern is so distinctive that, as is true for fingerprints, no two people's are the same, except for identical twins, which is why the technique is called DNA fingerprinting. It has been used to identify and convict criminals, as well as show that people who have been accused of crimes are innocent.

Genetic engineers experiment with altering, splicing, and rearranging genes. This research has resulted in medical breakthroughs in the treatment of diseases like diabetes and leukemia. Genetic engineering successes have also been seen in agricultural science. Agricultural breakthroughs like hybrid corn, disease-resistant grains, and higher quality livestock are all products of the principles of genetic engineering.

Population geneticists examine the breeding methods of farm animals and crops. They look at mutations that occur spontaneously or are introduced purposely to produce a marketable result.

Gene therapists hope to be able to treat disease and illness in the future by changing the genetic makeup of patients' cells. Gene therapy is a new and extremely experimental area of genetic science.

Education and Training

Study math, chemistry, biology, and physics in high school. English, writing, and computer courses will also be helpful for developing communication skills.

Words to Learn

cell the structural unit of which all body tissues are formed; there are billions of cells in the human body

chromosomes threadlike structures of nucleic acids and proteins that carry genes

DNA (deoxyribonucleic acid) the hereditary material of humans and many other living things

genes the units of heredity that are passed from parents to their children and control traits such as hair color, height, and so on

genetics the study of inheritance, or how living things resemble or differ from their ancestors

heredity the passing of traits from parents to their offspring

mutation a permanent change in a gene

nucleic acids chemical compounds in living cells and viruses

organism a single form of life such as a plant or animal

proteins the principal components of cells

In college, you should major in biology, chemistry, genetics, or another physical science. At public and private universities, colleges, and medical schools, genetic scientists almost always hold doctoral degrees and teach undergraduate and graduate courses in addition to doing research. Clinical geneticists usually earn an M.D. degree. Genetic counselors usually have master's degrees.

Tips for Success

To be a successful genetic scientist, you should

- be able to solve problems
- be a good communicator
- be patient
- be curious
- be attentive to detail
- be very organized
- be willing to continue to learn throughout your career

Earnings

Genetic scientists with a bachelor's degree hired by the federal government earned average starting salaries of $27,431 in 2010. Those with a master's degree earned starting salaries of either $33,979 or $41,563 depending on their qualifications. Doctoral degree holders earned $50,287 to start. Experienced geneticists employed by the federal government earned average salaries of $99,752 in 2009.

The average salary for genetic scientists working in private industry is approximately $75,000. Biotechnology firms pay higher salaries.

Outlook

Employment for genetic scientists should be excellent during the next decade. Interest in genetic research has exploded in the past decade, with numerous discoveries bringing greater attention to the exciting possibilities of finding genetic causes and cures for diseases.

As the need to understand human and animal biology and genetics and the fight to wipe out disease continue, demand

FOR MORE INFO

Visit the board's Web site for an overview of the career of genetic counselor.
American Board of Genetic Counseling
PO Box 14216
Lenexa, KS 66285-4216
913-895-4617
info@abgc.net
http://www.abgc.net

Contact the board for information on training for medical geneticists.
American Board of Medical Genetics
9650 Rockville Pike
Bethesda, MD 20814-3998
301-634-7315
abmg@abmg.org
http://www.abmg.org

Visit the society's Web site for information on educational programs and for the guide "Careers in Human Genetics."
American Society of Human Genetics
9650 Rockville Pike
Bethesda, MD 20814-3998
301-634-7300
http://www.ashg.org

For career information, including articles and books, contact
Biotechnology Industry Organization
1201 Maryland Avenue, SW, Suite 900
Washington, DC 20024-2149
202-962-9200
info@bio.org
http://www.bio.org

Visit the society's Web site for information on publications and membership for graduate students, as well as to read "Careers in Genetics."
Genetics Society of America
9650 Rockville Pike
Bethesda, MD 20814-3999
301-634-7300
http://www.genetics-gsa.org

For information on genetic counseling, contact
National Society of Genetic Counselors
401 North Michigan Avenue
Chicago, IL 60611-4255
312-321-6834
nsgc@nsgc.org
http://www.nsgc.org

for scientists will continue to increase. The world of criminal investigation is increasingly using genetics to win cases, drawing on genetic test results to identify culprits from bodily fluids or even a strand of hair.

Geologists

What Geologists Do

Geologists study the Earth—how it was formed, what it is made of, and how it is slowly changing. They gather rocks to study. Generally, geologists spend three to six months of the year making maps of certain areas and drilling deep holes in the Earth to obtain these rock samples. They study the rock samples in their laboratories under controlled temperatures and pressures. Finally, they organize the information they have gathered and write reports. These reports may be used to find groundwater, oil, minerals, and other natural resources.

Many geologists focus on a particular study of the Earth. For example, those who study the oceans are called *marine geologists.* Those who try to locate natural gas and oil deposits are called *petroleum geologists. Paleontologists* study the Earth's rock formations to determine the age of the Earth. *Engineering geologists* use their knowledge of geology to help solve problems that come up during the construction of roads, buildings, bridges, dams, and other structures. *Petrologists* study the origin and composition of igneous, metamorphic, and sedimentary rocks. *Stratigraphers* study the distribution and arrangement of sedimentary rock layers. This helps them to understand evolutionary changes in fossils and plants. *Geohydrologists* study the nature and distribution of water within the Earth. They often take part in studies that assess how a construction project will affect the environment. *Geomorphologists* study the Earth's surface and the processes, such as erosion and glaciation, that bring about changes. *Volcanologists* study volcanoes,

EXPLORING

- Visit Web sites about geology, such as Schoolyard Geology (http://education.usgs.gov/schoolyard), Kidipede: Geology for Kids (http://www.historyforkids.org/scienceforkids/geology), and KidsGeo.com (http://www.kidsgeo.com/geology-for-kids).
- Try to read as much as possible about geology and geologists. Here are some reading suggestions: *Geology Crafts for Kids: 50 Nifty Projects to Explore the Marvels of Planet Earth,* by Alan Anderson, Gwen Diehn, and Terry Krautwurst (Sterling Publishing Company, 1998); *Geology Rocks!: 50 Hands-On Activities to Explore the Earth,* by Cindy Blobaum and Michael Kline (Williamson Publishing Company, 1999); *The Practical Encyclopedia of Rocks & Minerals,* by John Farndon (Lorenz Books, 2006), and *The Illustrated Encyclopedia of Rocks of the World: A Practical Guide to Over 150 Igneous, Metamorphic and Sedimentary Rocks,* by John Farndon (Southwater, 2007).
- Amateur geological groups and local museums may have geology clubs you can join.
- Ask your science teacher or counselor to arrange an informational interview with a geologist.

their location, and their activity. *Glacial geologists* study glaciers and ice sheets.

The work of geologists can be demanding. They may travel to remote and rugged sites, often by helicopter or four-wheel-drive vehicle, and walk long distances. They may camp for extended periods of time in rough conditions away from their families. In addition, they spend long hours in the laboratory and preparing reports. In addition to scientific skills, geologists should have good communication skills, be organized, be able to think independently and creatively, and have physical stamina to do fieldwork.

Education and Training

Take a college preparatory curriculum while in high school. Such a curriculum will include computer science, history, English, and geography classes. Science and math classes are also important, particularly earth science, chemistry, and

All About Volcanoes on the Web

- Hawaii Volcanoes National Park
  http://www.nps.gov/havo
- How Volcanoes Work
  http://www.geology.sdsu.edu/
  how_volcanoes_work
- Volcano World
  http://volcano.oregonstate.edu
- Volcanoes: Can We Predict Volcanic Eruptions?
  http://www.learner.org/
  interactives/volcanoes

Words to Learn

erosion the wearing away of soil and other land features by water, wind, and human activities, such as farming and construction

fossil evidence of ancient life found in rocks and other substances

Geiger counter a device that detects radiation

glaciation the way in which land is changed by the movement of glaciers

global positioning system (GPS) a system of satellites that helps a user locate his or her exact position on Earth; GPS is also used in scientific research

groundwater water that is located beneath the surface of the Earth

A geologist stands in a trench dug to expose ancient layers of rock and vegetation. (Reed Saxon, AP Photo)

physics. Math classes should include algebra, trigonometry, and statistics.

To be a geologist, you need a bachelor's degree, usually in the physical and earth sciences. Positions in research, teaching, or exploration require a master's degree. Geologists who want to teach in a college or university or head a department in a business must earn a doctorate.

Many colleges, universities, and technical institutes offer programs in geology. Besides courses in geology, students study physics, chemistry, mathematics, English composition, eco-

Rock-Collecting Tips

Many people collect rocks as a hobby. Some gather them for color, such as agate with its bands of many hues. Others collect specimens for odd or beautiful shapes. Some look for imprints of fossils.

For people who want to do their own collecting, there are interesting rocks in every part of the country. Mountains, seashores, riverbanks, woods, and lava plains have an especially large number of different types of rocks. Many people simply pick up rocks on the surface of the ground. Others carry rock hammers, picks, shovels, and Geiger counters to help locate rocks. Hobbyists can buy rocks from specialty stores or scientific supply houses.

nomics, and foreign languages. Students who go on to graduate school will take advanced courses in geology and in the specialization of their choice.

Earnings

The U.S. Department of Labor reports that the average annual salary for geoscientists was $79,160 in 2008. New geologists earned $41,000 or less. Experienced geologists with advanced degrees earned more than $155,000. In the federal government, the average salary for geologists was $91,000 a year in 2008. Geologists who worked for state governments earned about $60,000 in 2008.

Outlook

Employment opportunities for geologists should be very good. Geologists will find jobs in the petroleum industry, but competition for those positions will be strong. Many of these jobs may

FOR MORE INFO

For information on geoscience careers, contact
American Geological Institute
4220 King Street
Alexandria, VA 22302-1502
703-379-2480
http://www.agiweb.org

For information on careers, contact
American Institute of Professional Geologists
1400 West 122nd Avenue, Suite 250
Westminster, CO 80234-3499
303-412-6205
aipg@aipg.org
http://www.aipg.org

For career information and profiles of women in geophysics, visit the association's Web site.
Association for Women Geoscientists
1400 West 122nd Avenue, Suite 250
Westminster, CO 80234-3499

office@awg.org
http://www.awg.org

For information on geology, contact
Association of Environmental and Engineering Geologists
PO Box 460518
Denver, CO 80246-0518
303-757-2926
aeg@aegweb.org
http://aegweb.org

For career information, contact
Geological Society of America
PO Box 9140
Boulder, CO 80301-9140
888-443-4472
gsaservice@geosociety.org
http://www.geosociety.org

For career and educational information about the geosciences, visit
U.S. Geological Survey
http://www.usgs.gov/education

be in foreign countries. Geologists may also find jobs in environmental protection and reclamation (cleanup). There will also be opportunities for geologists who work on highway, bridge, and other construction projects. Those with master's degrees who are familiar with computer modeling and the global positioning system will have the best employment opportunities. Knowing a foreign language will also help you land a job.

Geophysicists

What Geophysicists Do

Geology is the study of the history and composition of the Earth as recorded by rock formations and fossils. Physics deals with all forms of energy, the properties of matter, and the relationship between energy and matter.

Geophysicists study the physical structure of the Earth. This includes land surfaces, underground areas, and bodies of water such as oceans, lakes, and rivers. They use their knowledge to predict earthquakes, discover oil, and find safe places to build power plants. Their duties may include fieldwork, laboratory research, or college teaching.

Geophysicists often study environmental issues. For example, they may investigate whether an explosion designed to expose rich mineral deposits might also lead to an earthquake. They might examine the quality of underground water and how it affects a city's drinking supply.

Geophysicists usually specialize in one area of geophysics. For example, *seismologists* study earthquakes. They use seismographs and

EXPLORING

- You can find out more about geophysics by reading books on rocks and minerals, metals and metallurgy (the study of the physical and chemical properties of metals), the universe and space, and weather and climate. Here is one suggestion: *Planet Earth: What Planet Are You On?*, by Dan Green (Kingfisher, 2010).
- Develop hobbies that deal with radio, electronics, rock collecting, or map collecting.
- Visit the Society of Exploration Geophysicists kids' Web site, http://students.seg.org/kids.
- Talk to a geophysicist about his or her career.

other instruments to record the location of earthquakes and the vibrations they cause. They examine active fault lines and areas where earthquakes have occurred. *Hydrologists* study the movement and distribution of surface and underground waters. The information that they collect is applied to problems in flood control, crop production, soil and water conservation, irrigation, and inland water projects. Some hydrologists study glaciers. *Geodesists* measure the shape and size of the Earth to determine fixed points, positions, and elevations on or near the Earth's surface. *Geomagnetists* use specialized equipment to measure variations in the Earth's magnetic field from magnetic observatories and stations. *Applied geophysicists* use data gathered from the air and ground, as well as computers, to analyze the Earth's crust.

A geophysicist speaks about rock samples from two miles beneath the surface of the San Andreas Fault. (Paul Sakuma, AP Photo)

They look for oil and mineral deposits and try to find places where hazardous wastes can be safely disposed of. *Exploration geophysicists,* sometimes called *geophysical prospectors,* use seismic techniques to look for possible oil and gas deposits. *Volcanologists* study volcanoes, their location, and their activity. *Planetologists* study the makeup and atmosphere of the planets, the Moon, and other bodies in our solar system.

No matter what their area of specialization, geophysicists use the scientific principles of geology, chemistry, mathematics, physics, and engineering. Many of their instruments, such as the seismograph, take precise measurements of the Earth's physical characteristics, such as its electric, magnetic, and gravitational fields. *Field geophysicists* work outdoors in all kinds of weather. They often travel and work in remote areas. They may be away from home for long periods of time.

Major employers of geophysicists include the petroleum industry, mining companies, exploration and consulting firms, and research institutions, colleges and universities, and local, state, and federal government agencies. Major federal employees include the National Geodetic Survey, the U.S. Geological Survey, the National Geospatial-Intelligence Agency, and the Naval Oceanographic Office. A few geophysicists work as consultants.

Tips for Success

To be a successful geophysicist, you should

- **be very good at math and science**
- **have an interest in conducting experiments**
- **like solving problems**
- **enjoy working outdoors**
- **be able to work well as a member of a team**
- **be willing to continue to learn throughout your career**

Education and Training

Geophysicists should have a solid background in math and the physical and earth sciences. In high school you should take four years of math and courses in earth science, physics, and chemistry. Classes in mechanical drawing, history, and English are also highly recommended.

The best way to become a geophysicist is to get a bachelor's degree in geophysics, geoscience, or geology. A degree in physics, mathematics, or chemistry might be sufficient, but you should also take as many geology courses as you can. You will need a master's degree or doctorate in geophysics, geoscience, or geology for research or college teaching positions, and other positions with good advancement potential.

Helping Hands: Geoscientists Without Borders

You may be familiar with the organization Doctors Without Borders, a group of physicians and other health care workers who travel the world to volunteer their time to help people affected by poverty, war, and natural disasters. But did you know that there is now a similar organization for geoscientists? Geoscientists Without Borders, which is sponsored by the Society of Exploration Geophysicists (SEG), "applies geophysical technology to the needs of people from all areas of the globe through targeted projects designed to tangibly impact the community around them." The SEG Foundation provides grants to colleges and universities, which then send geoscience students and professionals around the world to conduct humanitarian and community geoscience projects. Clemson University, one of the first grant recipients, partnered with the Foundation for Economic Security (a nongovernmental organization in India) and the Indian Institute of Technology to help villagers in Madhya Pradesh, India, affected by drought (a shortage of water) and poor quality water. Participants searched for ways to capture water runoff from precipitation and increase supplies of groundwater during the dry season, developed irrigation plans for farming to put less stress on groundwater supplies, and used their training to search for new sources of groundwater. Visit http://www.seg.org/gwb for more information about Geoscientists Without Borders and its current projects.

FOR MORE INFO

For information on geoscience careers, contact
American Geological Institute
4220 King Street
Alexandria, VA 22302-1502
703-379-2480
http://www.agiweb.org

For industry information, contact
American Geophysical Union
2000 Florida Avenue, NW
Washington, DC 20009-1277
800-966-2481
http://www.agu.org

For information on careers in geophysics, contact
Society of Exploration Geophysicists
PO Box 702740
Tulsa, OK 74170-2740
918-497-5500
http://www.seg.org

For information on the geosciences and to read the online publication "Become a Geophysicist . . . A What?," visit the following Web sites:
U.S. Geological Survey
http://www.usgs.gov/education
http://earthquake.usgs.gov/learn/kids/become.php

Earnings

According to the U.S. Department of Labor, geoscientists (a career category that includes geophysicists, geologists, and other related workers) earned an average annual salary of $79,160 in 2008. Salaries ranged from less than $41,000 to more than $155,000 annually. In 2008, the average salary for a geophysicist working for the federal government was $91,030.

Outlook

Many geophysicists explore for oil and gas. Their employment opportunities depend on the strength of the petroleum industry. But even if job prospects in the oil industry are not good, there will continue to be jobs in teaching and other research areas. There is also demand for geophysicists to work in land and resource protection. Geophysicists who speak a foreign language and who are willing to work abroad will have the best job prospects.

Marine Biologists

What Marine Biologists Do

Marine biologists are a special type of oceanographer. They study the plants and animals that live in oceans. Marine biologists learn about the tens of thousands of different species that live in saltwater.

Marine biologists take sea voyages to study plants and animals in their natural environment. When they reach their destination, perhaps near a coral reef or other habitat, the scientists dive into the water to collect samples.

Because of the cold temperatures below the surface of the sea, marine biologists must wear wetsuits to keep warm. They use scuba gear to help them breathe under water. They may carry a tool called a slurp gun that can suck a fish into a specimen bag without hurting it. While underwater, biologists must watch out for dangerous fish and mammals such as sharks or stingrays. They take great care not to hurt the marine environment.

Marine biologists also gather specimens (samples of ocean life) from tidal pools along the shore. They may collect samples at the same time of day for days at a time. They keep samples from different pools separate and carefully write down the pool's location, the types of specimens taken, and their measurements. It is important to keep accurate records.

After they collect specimens, scientists keep them in a special portable aquarium tank on the ship. After returning to land, sometimes weeks or months later, marine biologists study the specimens in their laboratories. They might check the amount of oxygen in a sea turtle's bloodstream to learn how the turtles

60

EXPLORING

- Visit Web sites that focus on oceanography. Interesting sites include Careers in Oceanography, Marine Science, and Marine Biology (http://ocean.peterbrueggeman.com/career.html), MarineBio (http://www.marinebio.com), and Sea Grant Marine Careers (http://www.marinecareers.net).
- Read books about oceans, marine biology, animals, and careers in the field.
- Visit your local aquarium to learn about marine life and about the life of a marine biologist.
- If you live near an ocean you can collect shells and other specimens. Keep a notebook to record details about what you find and where.
- You can begin diving training while in high school. Between the ages of 10 and 14 you can earn a Junior Open Water Diver certification from PADI. This allows you to dive in the company of a certified adult. When you turn 15 you can upgrade your certification to Open Water Diver.
- Take up such hobbies as swimming, boating, snorkeling, or fishing.
- Turtles and fish make good pets for future marine biologists.
- Talk to a marine biologist about his or her career.

can stay underwater for so long. Or they might measure the blood chemistry of an arctic fish to discover how it can survive frigid (very cold) temperatures.

Marine biologists study changing conditions of the ocean, such as temperature or chemicals that have polluted the water. They try to see how those changes affect the plants and animals that live there. If certain species become extinct (die off) or are no longer safe to eat because of pollution, the world's food supply grows smaller.

Marine biologists study the remains of a dolphin that was stranded on a beach. (Larry Kolvoord, The Image Works)

The work of these scientists is also important for improving and managing sport and commercial fishing. Through underwater exploration, marine biologists have discovered that the world's coral reefs are being destroyed by humans. They have also charted the migration of whales and counted the decreasing numbers of certain species. They have seen dolphins being caught by accident in nets used by commercial fishing boats. By telling people about their discoveries through written reports and research papers, marine biologists sometimes help people and governments make changes that protect the environment.

In addition to conducting research in the field, marine biologists also teach marine biology at colleges and universities. Some marine biologists write books and articles about the field and appear as scientific experts in documentaries.

Marine biologists work for colleges and universities, government agencies (such as the National Oceanographic and Atmospheric Administration's Fisheries Service), drug companies that research marine sources for medicines, zoos and aquariums, and research institutions (such as the Scripps Institution of Oceanography).

Tips for Success

To be a successful marine biologist, you should

- enjoy asking questions to solve problems
- be able to observe small details carefully
- enjoy conducting research
- like math and science
- be a good diver
- enjoy being outdoors in all types of weather
- have good communication skills

Education and Training

If you want to be a marine biologist, you should like math and science. Biology, botany, and chemistry classes are important to take in high school. Although you can get a job as a marine biologist with a bachelor's degree, most marine biologists have a master's or doctoral degree. Typical core courses include introduction to biology, ecology and evolution biology, cell and molecular biology, marine ecology and evolution, genetic concepts, animal ecology, biochemistry of the ocean, microbiology, and field problems in marine biology. Elective courses include corals and coral reefs, animal evolution, aquatic pollution, and mathematical modeling.

DID YOU KNOW?

Octopus Facts

- The largest octopus is the North Pacific octopus (*Octopus dofleini*). It can grow to more than 30 feet and weighs more than 100 pounds.
- The smallest octopus is the Californian octopus (*Octopus micropyrsus*). It is only 3/8 inch to 1 inch in length.
- When threatened, octopuses often try to escape by releasing a cloud of purple-black ink to confuse the attacker.

Shark Facts

- Slow-growing sharks, such as the tope shark (*Galeorhinus galeus*) and piked dogfish (*Squalus acanthias*), can live more than 40 years.

- There are more than 375 species of sharks. Only 32 species of sharks have ever attacked people.
- On average, there are only 16 shark attacks a year in the United States. Great white (*Carcharodon carcharias*), tiger (*Galeocerdo cuvier*), and bull (*Carcharhinus leucas*) sharks are responsible for the most attacks on humans.
- The fastest shark is the shortfin mako (*Isurus oxyrinchus*), which can travel at speeds of up to 20 miles per hour.
- Sharks do not sleep. Instead they rest occasionally while staying awake.
- Sharks eat almost anything, including fish, crustaceans, mollusks, marine mammals, and other sharks.

Earnings

Salaries vary depending on how much education and experience you have. The average wildlife biologist earned about $55,000 in 2008, according to the U.S. Department of Labor. Those just starting out in the field earned less than $33,000. Those with doctorates in marine biology or a lot of experience earned more than $91,000 a year. Senior scientists or full professors at universities can earn more than $110,000 a year.

Outlook

Many people want to work as marine biologists—especially in top positions. Opportunities in research are especially hard to

FOR MORE INFO

For information on careers and marine science, contact the following organizations:

American Institute of Biological Sciences
1444 I Street, NW, Suite 200
Washington, DC 20005-6535
202-628-1500
http://www.aibs.org

American Society of Limnology and Oceanography
5400 Bosque Boulevard, Suite 680
Waco, TX 76710-4446
800-929-2756
http://www.aslo.org

This government agency is concerned with describing and predicting changes in the environment, as well as managing marine and coastal resources.
National Oceanographic and Atmospheric Administration
1401 Constitution Avenue, NW, Room 5128
Washington, DC 20230-0001

202-482-6090
noaa-outreach@noaa.gov
http://www.noaa.gov

For ocean news, contact
The Oceanography Society
PO Box 1931
Rockville, MD 20849-1931
301-251-7708
info@tos.org
http://www.tos.org

For information on diving instruction and certification, contact
PADI (Professional Association of Diving Instructors)
30151 Tomas Street
Rancho Santa Margarita, CA 92688-2125
800-729-7234
http://www.padi.com

find. Those who have advanced degrees and specialized knowledge in math and computer science will have the best chances for employment. Changes in the Earth's environment, such as global warming, will require more research and so create more jobs. Marine biologists should be able to find jobs managing the world's fisheries, making medicines from marine organisms, and cultivating (growing) marine food alternatives, such as seaweed and plankton.

Meteorologists

What Meteorologists Do

The lives and work of many people depend on the weather research conducted by *meteorologists*. Airline pilots, ship captains, farmers, and everyday citizens all rely on the careful and detailed work of meteorologists. Meteorologists help people know how to prepare for the weather outside.

Meteorologists study weather conditions to predict, or forecast, changes in the weather. They gather information daily, and sometimes hourly, from weather satellites above the Earth. They use this information about the atmosphere to make charts and maps that show regional and local temperatures, rainfall, winds, pressure areas, and cloud coverage.

To make their predictions, meteorologists gather weather information from many sources. In addition to weather satellites and weather radar, information is also sent from remote sensors and observers in many parts of the world. Meteorologists use advanced computer models of the world's atmosphere to help with their long-range, short-range, and local forecasts.

Most meteorologists specialize in one area. *Weather forecasters* make up the largest group of meteorologists. Many forecasters work at radio and television studios. They forecast short- and long-range weather during news shows.

There are many other types of meteorologists. *Dynamic meteorologists* study the physical laws related to air currents. *Physical meteorologists* study the physical nature of the atmosphere, including its chemical composition and electrical, acoustical, and optical properties. *Environmental meteorologists*

66

EXPLORING

- Read books and magazines about weather. Here are two suggestions: *Scholastic Atlas of Weather,* by Marie-Anne Legault (Scholastic, 2004); *Experiments with Weather,* by Salvatore Tocci (Children's Press, 2004); and *Meteorology Today: An Introduction to Weather, Climate, and the Environment,* 9th edition, by C. Donald Ahrens (Brooks Cole, 2008).
- Visit weather Web sites (see Surf the Web).
- Learn as much as you can about weather, from the types of clouds in the sky, to thunderstorms and tornadoes, to hurricanes, microbursts, and more.
- The American Meteorological Society offers a great career guide at its Web site, http://www.ametsoc.org/atmoscareers.
- Learn how to take basic weather readings such as temperature, wind speed, barometric pressure, and snow or rain totals.
- Ask your science teacher to arrange an informational interview with a meteorologist.

study air pollution, global warming, ozone depletion, water shortages, and other environmental problems and write impact statements about their findings. *Industrial meteorologists* work in a variety of private industries. They focus on such problems as smoke control and air pollution. *Synoptic meteorologists* study large-scale patterns responsible for daily weather as well as find new ways to forecast weather events by using mathematical models and computers. *Flight meteorologists* fly in aircraft to study hurricanes and other weather phenomena. *Climatologists* study past weather conditions of a region over a long period of time. They try to predict future weather patterns

DID YOU KNOW?

- Tornadoes move at an average speed of 30 miles per hour, but can also be stationary (motionless) or move as fast as 70 miles per hour.
- Tornadoes can occur at any time of the day, but most often happen between 3 P.M. and 9 P.M.
- The most violent tornadoes can have wind speeds of more than 250 miles per hour.
- About 70 people are killed in the United States by tornadoes each year. Approximately 1,500 people are injured.

Source: National Oceanographic and Atmospheric Administration

Surf the Web

- AccuWeather.com
  http://www.accuweather.com
- National Weather Service
  http://www.nws.noaa.gov
- The Weather Channel
  http://www.weather.com
- Weather Dude
  http://www.wxdude.com
- Weather Underground
  http://www.wunderground.com

for the region. Some meteorologists do not forecast at all. They teach in colleges and universities.

The National Weather Service (NWS) employs most meteorologists. The U.S. Department of Defense, including the armed forces, employs the next greatest number. Other meteorologists work for weather consulting firms, airline companies, radio and television stations, engineering service firms, and computer and data processing services. Companies that design and make meteorological instruments, aircraft, and missiles also hire meteorologists. Others teach in colleges and universities.

Successful meteorologists are organized, have strong technical skills, work well with others, and have excellent knowledge of meteorology. They should also have strong communication skills, especially if they work in broadcasting. Other important skills are the ability to work well under pressure and a willingness to work a variety of shifts, including nights and weekends.

Education and Training

In high school, you should take as many classes as you can in the physical sciences.

All meteorologists need at least a bachelor's degree. Many

of the best jobs, though, require a master's or a doctoral degree. The best research jobs and nearly all teaching jobs in colleges and universities go to meteorologists who have advanced graduate training.

Earnings

The U.S. Department of Labor reports that median annual earnings of atmospheric scientists (a career that includes meteorologists) were $81,290 in 2008. Salaries ranged from less than $39,000 to more than $127,000. The mean salary for meteorologists employed by the federal government was $93,661 in 2009. Broadcast meteorologists earn between $16,000 and $1 million or more depending on where they work. Experienced broadcast meteorologists average $50,000 a year.

A meteorologist at the National Weather Service looks at weather maps generated from satellite data. (David R. Frazier, The Image Works)

FOR MORE INFO

For information on careers and education, contact
American Meteorological Society
45 Beacon Street
Boston, MA 02108-3693
617-227-2425
amsinfo@ametsoc.org
http://www.ametsoc.org

This government agency is concerned with describing and predicting changes in the environment, as well as managing marine and coastal resources.
National Oceanographic and Atmospheric Administration
1401 Constitution Avenue, NW,
Room 5128
Washington, DC 20230-0001
202-482-6090

noaa-outreach@noaa.gov
http://www.noaa.gov and http://www.ncep.noaa.gov

For a list of schools with degree programs in meteorology or atmospheric science, visit the association's Web site.
National Weather Association
228 West Millbrook Road
Raleigh, NC 27609-4304
919-845-1546
http://www.nwas.org

To learn more about the weather, visit the NWS Web site.
National Weather Service (NWS)
1325 East West Highway
Silver Spring, MD 20910-3280
http://www.nws.noaa.gov

Outlook

Employment for meteorologists should be good during the next decade, but competition will be very strong for jobs since people consider meteorology an exciting field.

Opportunities for meteorologists in private industry will be better than in the federal government. Private weather consulting firms are able to provide more detailed information than the NWS to weather-sensitive industries, such as agriculture, commodities trading, and utilities, transportation, and construction firms.

Employment will be fair for broadcast meteorologists. The best opportunities will be available to those with certification and strong broadcasting skills.

Oceanographers

What Oceanographers Do

Oceanographers are scientists who study the oceans. They conduct experiments and gather information about the water, plant and animal life, and the ocean floor. They study the motion of waves, currents (a strong flow of water within a larger body of water), and tides (the regular rise and fall of water in an ocean or lake). They also look at water temperature, the chemical makeup of the ocean water, and pollution levels at different depths of the oceans.

Oceanographers use several inventions specially designed for long- and short-term underwater observation. They use deep-sea equipment, such as submarines and observation tanks. Underwater devices called bathyspheres allow an oceanographer to stay underwater for several hours or even days. For short observations or to explore areas such as underwater caves, scientists use deep-sea and scuba diving gear that straps onto the body to supply them with oxygen.

Oceanographers do most of their work out on the water. While at sea, they gather the scientific information that they need. Then they spend long periods of time in offices, laboratories, or libraries studying the data. Oceanographers use information such as water temperature changes between the surface and the lower depths to predict droughts and monsoons (strong seasonal rains). Droughts are periods of time when there is little or no rain. Monsoons are heavy rains that can cause major flooding and damage.

Most oceanographers specialize in one of four areas.

EXPLORING

- Visit Web sites that focus on oceanography. Interesting sites include Careers in Oceanography, Marine Science, and Marine Biology (http://ocean.peterbrueggeman.com/career.html), MarineBio.org (http://www.marinebio.com), and Sea Grant Marine Careers (http://www.marinecareers.net).
- If you live near a coastal region, it will be easier to learn about oceans and ocean life. Read all you can about rocks, minerals, and aquatic life. If you live or travel near an oceanography research center,

such as Woods Hole Oceanographic Institution (http://www.whoi.edu) on Cape Cod in Massachusetts, spend some time studying its exhibits.
- If you do not live near the ocean, try to find summer camps or programs that make trips to coastal areas. Learn all you can about the geology, atmosphere, and plant and animal life of the area where you live.
- Ask a counselor or teacher to help arrange an informational interview with an oceanographer.

Those who study ocean plants and animals are called *biological oceanographers* or *marine biologists.* They collect information on the behavior and activities of the wildlife in a specific area of the ocean.

Physical oceanographers study ocean temperature and the atmosphere above the water. They study the greenhouse effect, or the warming of the planet's surface. They calculate the movement of warm water (known as a current) through the oceans to help meteorologists predict weather patterns.

Geological oceanographers study the ocean floor. They use instruments that monitor the ocean floor and the minerals

DID YOU KNOW?

- Oceans cover about 71 percent of the planet's surface—or 140 million square miles.
- Approximately 80 percent of all life on Earth lives in the ocean.
- Ocean depth averages 2.3 miles. The greatest known depth of any ocean is in the Challenger Deep of the Mariana Trench in the Pacific Ocean, about 250 miles southwest of Guam. Recorded echo soundings show a maximum depth of 36,198 feet.
- The ocean's complicated food webs support more life by weight and a greater diversity of animals than any other ecosystem.
- The oceans have vast stores of valuable minerals, including nickel, iron, manganese, copper, cobalt, and gold. In fact, it is estimated that there are nearly 20 million tons of gold in the world's oceans.
- The surface temperature of oceans ranges from about 86°F at the equator to about 29°F near the poles. The world's warmest water is in the Persian Gulf, where surface temperatures of 96°F have been recorded.
- Less than 10 percent of the deepest parts of the ocean, called the abyss, have been explored.
- More than 3.5 billion people rely on the ocean as their main source of food.

Source: SavetheSea.org

found there from a far distance. In areas where the ocean is too deep for any human-made equipment to go, they use remote sensors.

Chemical oceanographers, also known as *geochemical oceanographers,* study the chemical makeup of ocean water and the ocean floor. They study pollution problems and possible chemical causes for plant and animal diseases in a particular region of the water. Chemical oceanographers are called in after oil spills to check the level of damage to the water and ecosystem (a group of organisms living together with nonliving components).

About 17 percent of oceanographers work for federal or state governments. Federal employers of oceanographers include the National Science Foundation; Departments of Commerce, Defense, Energy, and Interior; National Aeronautics and Space Administration; Environmental Protection Agency; Biological Resources Discipline of the U.S. Geological Survey; Naval Oceanographic Office; Naval Research Laboratory; and Office of Naval Research, among others. State governments often employ oceanographers in environmental agencies or state-funded research projects. About 40 percent of oceanographers work for colleges or universities as teachers and researchers. The remaining oceanographers work for private industries such as nonprofit organizations, oil and gas extraction companies, and industrial firms.

Education and Training

Science courses, including geology, biology, and chemistry, and math classes, such as algebra, trigonometry, and statistics, are especially important to take in high school. Because your work will involve a great deal of research and documentation, take English classes to improve your research and communication skills. In addition, take computer science classes because you will use computers throughout your professional life.

To become an oceanographer, you will need at least a bachelor's degree in chemistry, biology, geology, or physics. For most research or teaching positions, you will need a master's degree or doctoral degree in oceanography.

Tips for Success

To be a successful oceanographer, you should

- have a strong interest in science, especially the physical and earth sciences
- be curious
- enjoy being outdoors
- enjoy observing nature and performing experiments
- like reading, researching, and writing
- have good communication skills
- be able to work well with others

Earnings

Students graduating with a bachelor's degree in geology and related sciences were offered an average starting salary of $40,786 in 2007, according to the National Association of Colleges and Employers. Salaries for geoscientists (a category that includes oceanographers) ranged from less than $42,000 to more than $155,000 in 2008, with a median of $79,160, according to the U.S. Department of Labor. The average salary for experienced oceanographers working for the federal government was about $105,000 in 2009.

Outlook

Employment for all geoscientists (including oceanographers) is expected to be good. Although the field of marine science is growing, researchers specializing in the popular field of biological oceanography will face competition for available positions and research funding. However, because more people want to understand and protect the environment there will be more jobs available. There will be more jobs for oceanographers who study global climate change and fisheries science, conduct marine biomedical and pharmaceutical research, and study the ocean as a source of renewable energy. Oceanographers who can speak a foreign language and who don't mind working outside the United States will have good job prospects.

In general, oceanographers who also have training in other sciences or in engineering will probably have better opportunities for jobs than those with training limited to oceanography.

FOR MORE INFO

For education and career information, contact the following organizations:

Acoustical Society of America
2 Huntington Quadrangle, Suite 1NO1
Melville, NY 11747-4502
516-576-2360
asa@aip.org
http://asa.aip.org

American Geophysical Union
2000 Florida Avenue, NW
Washington, DC 20009-1277
800-966-2481
http://www.agu.org

This organization for diving scientists stresses diving safety.

American Academy of Underwater Scientists
Dauphin Island Sea Lab
101 Bienville Boulevard
Dauphin Island, AL 36528-4603
251-861-7504
aaus@disl.org
http://www.aaus.org

The Education section of the AIBS Web site has information on a number of careers in biology.

American Institute of Biological Sciences (AIBS)
1444 I Street, NW, Suite 200
Washington, DC 20005-6535
202-628-1500
admin@aibs.org
http://www.aibs.org

For information about careers, education, and publications, contact

American Society of Limnology and Oceanography
5400 Bosque Boulevard, Suite 680
Waco, TX 76710-4446
800-929-2756
http://www.aslo.org

For information on how to join the MTS Club (for students in grades 6–12), contact

Marine Technology Society (MTS)
5565 Sterrett Place, Suite 108
Columbia, MD 21044-2606
410-884-5330
http://www.mtsociety.org

This government agency is concerned with describing and predicting changes in the environment, as well as managing marine and coastal resources.

National Oceanographic and Atmospheric Administration
1401 Constitution Avenue, NW, Room 5128
Washington, DC 20230-0001
202-482-6090
noaa-outreach@noaa.gov
http://www.noaa.gov

For ocean news, contact

The Oceanography Society
PO Box 1931
Rockville, MD 20849-1931
301-251-7708
info@tos.org
http://www.tos.org

Paleontologists

What Paleontologists Do

Paleontologists study rocks and fossils. Fossils are the remains or traces of prehistoric plants and animals that were preserved in the rocks of the Earth.

Paleontologists study rock formations for a variety of reasons. They do this to learn more about the history of life on Earth, the placement of land and water, and the location of important substances, such as oil, gas, and coal. Rocks give clues about ancient environments and climates.

Fossils help paleontologists figure out the age of rocks on the Earth. Once the age of the fossil is determined, then scientists can estimate the age of the surrounding rock. Paleontologists also study fossils to figure out the age of a certain type of plant or animal. They determine when it lived, and compare it to similar plants and animals from various time periods. This helps them trace the animal or plant's evolution to see how it has changed or adapted from one time period to the next.

Paleontologists spend a lot of time in laboratories. They also travel all over the world to work in the field—sometimes for months at a time—collecting specimens to examine. Fieldwork is sometimes demanding. It takes patience to gather and interpret detailed information about the Earth. Paleontologists use dynamite and jackhammers, masonry hammers, chisels, putty knives, trowels, sifters, and soft-bristled paintbrushes. And they always carry a notebook and pen or pencil to make detailed notes.

Most paleontologists work in colleges and universities. They also work in museums, with government research projects,

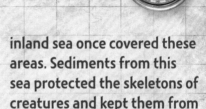

EXPLORING

- Contact local geology or natural history museums about field trips that are open to the public. Museums may also be able to direct you to local rock- or fossil-collecting clubs.
- Contact your state geological society for information about fossils and fossil-hunting opportunities in your area.
- The Midwest and Great Plains states are especially rich in fossil beds. This is because an inland sea once covered these areas. Sediments from this sea protected the skeletons of creatures and kept them from being moved about.
- Professional geology societies publish brochures on fossil hunting and the kinds of fossils available in different areas.
- Ask a counselor or teacher to help arrange an informational interview with a paleontologist.

and in the petroleum industry. Some paleontologists are self-employed, offering their expertise as consultants.

Education and Training

In high school, take courses in science and math, including advanced classes in biology, chemistry, algebra, and trigonometry. Paleontologists also use computers, so take courses in computers and programming. English and speech classes will help you prepare your findings for publication and presentation. Foreign language classes will also be valuable, as you may need to do research in other countries.

Paleontology is a subspecialty in the field of geology. Paleontologists usually study geology in college, although a few major in such fields as botany or zoology. After college, you go on to study paleontology in graduate school.

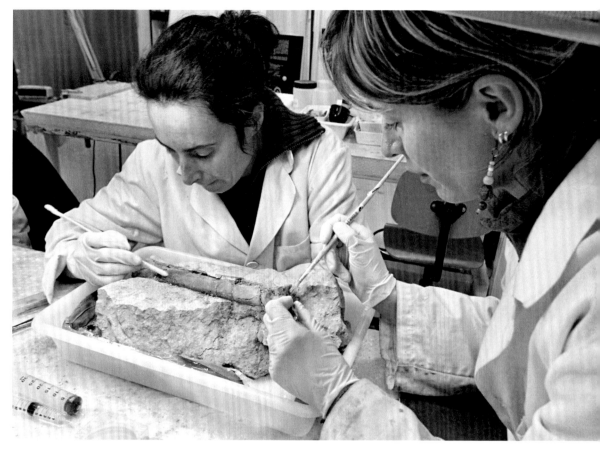

Paleontologists clean fossils in a lab. (Mike Calvo, V&W, The Image Works)

Most paleontologists earn a doctoral degree (Ph.D.). Those with master's degrees may be able to find work as technicians, either as *preparators* (a person who prepares scientific specimens), collections managers, or lab supervisors. Those who wish to do research, exploration, college-level teaching, or museum work will need a doctorate.

Earnings

Geoscientists (a career category that includes paleontologists) earned median annual salaries of $79,160, according to the U.S. Department of Labor. Salaries ranged from less than $41,000 to $155,000 or more. Geoscientists who are employed by the federal government earn higher salaries than those who work for state government agencies and private companies.

Outlook

There are few job openings for paleontologists, so the competition is stiff. More paleontologists graduate every year than there are positions open for them. There are also fewer educational

Helping Hands: Paul Sereno

Some people call Paul Sereno a real-life Indiana Jones. Sereno is a world-famous paleontologist. He travels the world searching for the bones of dinosaurs. He has discovered the remains of dinosaurs on five continents. These range from *Suchomimus*, a fish-eating dinosaur; to *Afrovenator*, a 27-foot-long meat-eater, to *Carcharodontosaurus*, a gigantic meat-eating dinosaur. In addition to discovering dinosaur bones, Sereno and his team found the remains of *Sarcosuchus*, the largest crocodile that ever lived on earth. SuperCroc (http://www.supercroc.org), as it has come to be nicknamed, was 40 feet long. It was so big that it could eat dinosaurs!

Dinosaur-hunting and other scientific expeditions are fun but very expensive. Sometimes kids from families without a lot of money don't have a way to participate in such activities. In 1999, Paul Sereno and his wife founded Project Exploration, which offers a variety of programs that help young people—especially girls—explore the natural sciences alongside scientists in many fields. Opportunities include a Junior Paleontologist summer program; Sisters4Science, "a year-round after-school and field program that combines science exploration with leadership development"; and the Girls' Health and Science Day conference. Visit http://www.projectexploration.org for more information on Paul Sereno and Project Exploration.

Sources: PaulSereno.org, *National Geographic*, Project Exploration

DID YOU KNOW?

- The first dinosaurs appeared on Earth about 230 million years ago.
- The largest dinosaur was *Brachiosaurus*. It was "about the length of two large school buses and the height of a four-story building (about 40–50 feet)."

- The smallest dinosaur was *Compsognathus*, which was slightly larger than a chicken.
- It is estimated that dinosaurs became extinct about 65 million years ago.

Source: U.S. Geological Survey

opportunities, as colleges are closing geology departments in order to cut costs. To increase opportunities for employment, paleontologists will have to train in other areas, such as zoology or botany.

FOR MORE INFO

For information on geoscience careers, contact
American Geological Institute
4220 King Street
Alexandria, VA 22302-1502
703-379-2480
http://www.agiweb.org

For career information, contact
Geological Society of America
PO Box 9140
Boulder, CO 80301-9140
888-443-4472
gsaservice@geosociety.org
http://www.geosociety.org

For general information about paleontology, contact
Paleontological Research Institution
1259 Trumansburg Road
Ithaca, NY 14850-1313
607-273-6623
http://www.museumoftheearth.org

For information on careers, contact
Society of Vertebrate Paleontology
111 Deer Lake Road, Suite 100
Deerfield, IL 60015-4943
847-480-9095
http://www.vertpaleo.org

Pharmacologists

What Pharmacologists Do

Pharmacologists are scientists who study how drugs, chemicals, and other materials affect human beings and other animals. Some pharmacologists develop and test new drugs for doctors to use in treating disease. Others test chemicals, pollutants, and other materials found in homes, farms, and factories to see how they affect living things.

Pharmacologists in drug research study the effects of medical substances on the human body. Their goal is to find out about the good effects and the possibly bad side effects that a drug may have. Using this information, pharmacologists can tell drug companies the best way to manufacture the drug. They tell physicians when and how the drug should be given to patients.

Pharmacologists who specialize in testing chemicals, pollutants, and other substances in the environment and in food look for possible harmful effects. They do research on industrial materials, pesticides, food preservatives and colorings (materials that keep food fresh and artificially add color to them), and even on common household items such as paints, aerosol sprays, and cleaning fluids to find out whether they are safe to use.

Pharmacologists do most of their research in laboratories using laboratory animals, plants, and tissue samples from animals and human donors. *Clinical pharmacologists* test drugs on human subjects. Some pharmacologists specialize in particular parts of the body. For example, *neuropharmacologists* study drugs that affect the nervous system. *Cardiovascular pharmacologists* study drugs for the heart, lungs, and circulatory

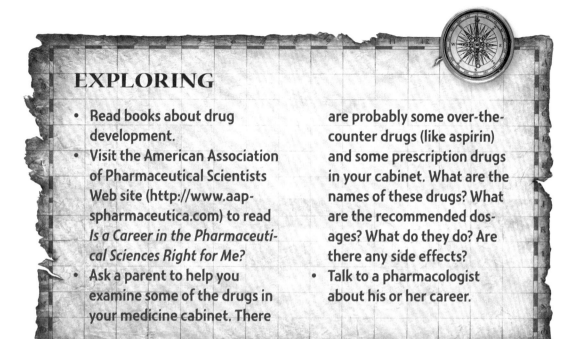

EXPLORING

- Read books about drug development.
- Visit the American Association of Pharmaceutical Scientists Web site (http://www.aapspharmaceutica.com) to read *Is a Career in the Pharmaceutical Sciences Right for Me?*
- Ask a parent to help you examine some of the drugs in your medicine cabinet. There

are probably some over-the-counter drugs (like aspirin) and some prescription drugs in your cabinet. What are the names of these drugs? What are the recommended dosages? What do they do? Are there any side effects?

- Talk to a pharmacologist about his or her career.

systems. *Behavioral pharmacologists* specialize in the effects of drugs on mood and behavior. *Moluecular pharmacologists* study the interactions of drug molecules and cells. *Biochemical pharmacologists* use biochemistry, cell biology, and physiology to determine how drugs interact and influence the chemical makeup of an organism.

Pharmacologists work as teachers at medical, dental, veterinary, or pharmacy schools. Others work as researchers in large hospitals, medical centers, or research institutes. They also work for government agencies involved in research such as the National Institutes of Health, Centers for Disease Control, the Environmental Protection Agency, and the Food and Drug Administration.

Education and Training

To be a pharmacologist, you must have a good background in science and math. In high school and college, you should take as many courses as possible in basic science, chemistry, biology,

Tips for Success

To be a successful pharmacologist, you should

- enjoy science
- like solving problems
- have excellent communication skills
- be curious
- have patience
- be able to work well both alone and with others

organic chemistry, and math. You should also take English so that you will be able to write research reports.

Your first step in becoming a pharmacologist is to earn a bachelor's degree in chemistry, pharmacy, or one of the biological sciences. All pharmacologists have a doctorate. Earning a doctorate in pharmacology requires four to five years of study after college, usually at a medical school or pharmacy school. Because pharmacology is so closely related to the practice of medicine, many pharmacologists are also medical doctors or veterinarians.

Earnings

Average salaries for pharmacologists were $124,600 in 2008, according to a survey by the American Association of Phar-

Profile: François Magendie (1783–1855)

Many consider François Magendie to be the father of experimental pharmacology. The French physiologist conducted fact-based studies of the poisons strychnine and carbon monoxide and the muscle relaxant curare, among other substances. He made other important findings relating to digestion and the workings of the human heart and nervous and circulatory systems. His discoveries helped the pharmaceutical industry develop life-saving drugs and the medical world to better understand the human body.

Sources: French Ministry of Culture, Claude Moore Health Sciences Library

FOR MORE INFO

To learn more about pharmacology and read news of interest to those in the field, visit the AAPS Web site.

American Association of Pharmaceutical Scientists (AAPS)
2107 Wilson Boulevard, Suite 700
Arlington, VA 22201-3042
703-243-2800
http://www.aapspharmaceutica.com

For information about careers and educational opportunities for students, contact

American Society for Pharmacology and Experimental Therapeutics
9650 Rockville Pike
Bethesda, MD 20814-3995
301-634-7135
info@aspet.org
http://www.aspet.org

maceutical Scientists. Salaries ranged from less than $90,000 to $150,000 or more. Pharmaceutical scientists working in industry earned the highest salaries, $120,000 a year. Pharmacologists with the highest salaries are either those who supervise teams of people in large laboratories or senior faculty in colleges and universities. Bonuses, especially for those in industry, can increase yearly earnings considerably.

Outlook

There should be many jobs for pharmacologists during the next decade. There will be more and more demand for health care services and products in the coming years, especially as the elderly population increases. There will be plenty of jobs for pharmacologists who develop new drugs. They will play an important part in fighting diseases such as AIDS and cancer.

Physicists

What Physicists Do

Physicists try to understand the laws of nature and learn how to use these laws in ways that will help us in our daily lives. Some teach in high schools and colleges, some work for the federal government, and some work for industrial laboratories. Wherever they work, physicists spend a great deal of time doing research, conducting experiments, and studying the results.

Physicists are concerned with the special properties of matter (solids, liquids, and gases) and energy (the capacity of being active; power like heat or electricity that can be used). *Theoretical physicists* try to understand how matter and energy work. For example, they may study electrical or nuclear energy, try to define the laws of each, and then write them up in mathematical formulas. *Experimental physicists* perform experiments that test exactly what various kinds of matter and energy do. Then they try to come up with practical ways to use them. For example, they may work in the communications industries, such as television, telephone, radio, or Internet, to invent technologies for better pictures or better sound.

Physicists work in many areas. Physicists may specialize in mechanics, heat, optics (light), acoustics (sound), electricity and magnetism, electronics, particle physics (atoms and molecules), nuclear physics, or physics of fluids. Others work with engineers to find the best ways to build bridges and dams. Others conduct experiments for petroleum companies, to find better ways to obtain, refine, and use crude oil. Physicists are important to

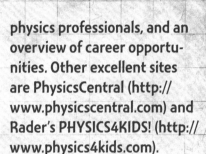

EXPLORING

- Read books about physics. Here are some suggestion: *Physics: Why Matter Matters!*, by Dan Green (Kingfisher, 2008); *The Manga Guide to Physics*, by Hideo Nitta and Keita Takatsu (No Starch Press, 2009); *Flying Circus of Physics*, 2nd edition, by Jearl Walker (Wiley, 2006); and *George's Secret Key to the Universe* and *George's Cosmic Treasure Hunt*, both by Stephen and Lucy Hawking (Simon & Schuster Children's Publishing, 2009).
- Visit the American Physical Society's Web site for students, http://www.aps.org/careers/student. It features information on recommended middle and high school classes, interviews with physics professionals, and an overview of career opportunities. Other excellent sites are PhysicsCentral (http://www.physicscentral.com) and Rader's PHYSICS4KIDS! (http://www.physics4kids.com).
- Ask your science teacher to assign some physics experiments.
- Join a science club or start one at your school.
- Enter a project in a science fair. If your school does not sponsor science fairs, you may find fairs sponsored by your school district, state, or a science society.
- Talk to a physicist about his or her career. Ask your science teacher or counselor to help you set up an interview.

the space program. They try to figure out what outer space is actually like, and they design and test spaceships. These specialized physicists are known as *astrophysicists.*

Although biology and geology are separate sciences in their own right, the concepts of physics can also be applied directly to them. Where this application has been made, a new series of

Famous Physics Labs

These are some of the Department of Energy's research and development facilities:

- Brookhaven National Laboratory (http://www.bnl.gov/world) in Upton, Long Island, New York, is mainly involved in studies of nuclear physics. It also does chemical, biological, environmental, medical imaging, neuroscience, and nonproliferation research.
- Fermi National Accelerator Laboratory (http://www.fnal.gov) in Batavia, Illinois, conducts research in high-energy physics.

- Lawrence Berkeley National Laboratory (http://www.lbl.gov) in Berkeley, California, conducts research in fundamental studies of the universe, quantitative biology, nanoscience, new energy systems and environmental solutions, and integrated computing.
- Los Alamos National Laboratory (http://www.lanl.gov) in Los Alamos, New Mexico, conducts research in nuclear weapons and energy, cryogenic physics, space sciences, molecular biology, and metallurgy.

sciences has developed. To separate them from their parent sciences, they are known by such names as biophysics (the physics of living things) and geophysics (the physics of the Earth). Similarly, the sciences of chemistry and physics sometimes overlap in subject matter as well as in viewpoint and procedure, creating physical chemistry.

All physicists must have keen powers of observation, have a strong curiosity about the world around them, and enjoy solving problems. They are also detail oriented, precise, and good communicators. Physicists should have patience and be able to work alone or on research teams. They should also be willing to continue to learn throughout their careers.

Education and Training

In high school, take as many mathematics courses (algebra, advanced algebra, and calculus) as you can, and explore as many of the sciences as possible. English skills are important because you must write up your results, communicate with other scientists, and lecture on your findings. In addition, get as much experience as possible using computers.

There are some jobs available for physicists with only a bachelor's degree. If you have a bachelor's degree, you may be able to find a basic research job. If you have a teaching certificate, you can teach at a high school.

Most physicists will need to go on for further education if they want to advance in the field. The more challenging and rewarding jobs go to physicists who have master's degrees and doctorates. Many of the most able physicists go on to complete postdoctoral education.

DID YOU KNOW?

Where Physicists Work

- Federal government (U.S. Departments of Defense, Energy, Health and Human Services, and Commerce, national laboratories, and for the National Aeronautics and Space Administration)
- State government agencies
- Private companies
- Colleges and universities
- Hospitals

Earnings

The median salary for physicists was $102,890 in 2008, according to the U.S. Department of Labor. Salaries ranged from less than $57,000 to $159,000 or more. Physicists employed by the federal government had mean annual earnings of $108,020. The most highly paid physicists have doctoral degrees and many years of experience.

Outlook

Employment for physicists should be good during the next decade. Increases in government research, particularly in the De-

FOR MORE INFO

For employment statistics and information on jobs and career planning, contact

American Institute of Physics
One Physics Ellipse
College Park, MD 20740-3843
301-209-3100
aipinfo@aip.org
http://www.aip.org

For information on educational requirements and careers, contact

American Physical Society
One Physics Ellipse
College Park, MD 20740-3844
301-209-3200
http://www.aps.org

Fermilab is a U.S. Department of Energy research and development laboratory. Visit the following Web sites to learn more about the laboratory and precollege education programs.

Fermi National Accelerator Laboratory
Education Office
Fermilab MS 226
Box 500
Batavia, IL 60510-5011
630-840-3092
http://www.fnal.gov and http://www.fnal.gov/pub/education/k-12_programs.html

partments of Defense and Energy, will create more opportunities for physicists. Physics-related research in the private sector is expected to decline. The U.S. Department of Labor predicts that there will be many opportunities for graduate-level physicists outside of traditional physics fields. They will have job titles such as computer programmer, computer software engineer, or systems analyst or developer, rather than physicist. Those with just a bachelor's degree in physics will find opportunities as high school physics teachers and in occupational areas such as mathematics, computer science, engineering, environmental science, and finance.

Science and Medical Writers

What Science and Medical Writers Do

Science and medical writers translate technical, medical, and scientific information so it can be easily understood by "regular" people, as well as professionals in the field. They research, interpret, write, and edit scientific and medical information. Their work appears in books, technical studies and reports, magazine articles, newspapers, newsletters, and on Web sites. It also may be used in radio and television broadcasts.

Educational publishers hire science and medical writers to write or edit educational materials for the medical profession. Or that same publisher may may hire writers to write online articles or interactive courses that are distributed over the Internet.

A science or medical writer may write medical information and consumer publications about a new drug made by a pharmaceutical company. Research facilities employ them to edit reports or write about their scientific or medical studies. Science and medical writers may work as *public information officers.* They write press releases that

EXPLORING

- Read books and magazines about science and medical topics. Your school or local librarian should be able to suggest some good titles.
- Write a short article for your parents or friends that summarizes a medical or science news story you read about online or in a newspaper or magazine.
- Ask your science or health teacher to arrange an informational interview with a science or medical writer.
- Hone your writing skills by writing as much as possible.

inform the public about the latest scientific or medical research findings. A researcher's press release is a short summary of the most important points of scientists' findings. Press releases are distributed to people who will spread this information to others.

To be a good writer who covers subjects in detail, science and medical writers must ask a lot of questions and enjoy hunting for information that might improve the article. They do hours of research on the Internet or in libraries. Sometimes writers interview professionals such as doctors, pharmacists, scientists, engineers, managers, and others who know a lot about the subject. They may have to include graphs, photos, or historical facts. If they write stories that appear on the Internet, they may shoot video, take photos, or create drawings that help people understand the story better. This type of creative work may also be done by *science and medical videographers, photographers, or illustrators.*

Words to Learn

byline a line that credits the name of a writer of an article

online publication a resource that is published on the Internet

portfolio a collection of one's work that serves as a work sample for a person seeking a job

print publication a newspaper, magazine, book, or other publication that is printed on paper

stringer a freelance photographer or reporter who works for a book publisher or newspaper or magazine publisher on an as-needed basis

syndicate an organization that sells special articles or features for publication by many newspapers or magazines

Some medical and science writers specialize in their subject matter. For instance, a medical writer may write only about heart disease and become known as the best writer in that subject. Another may focus on covering scientific developments relating to cancer. Science writers may limit their writing or focus on only one subject such as air pollution or space flight.

If you are considering a career as a medical or science writer, you should enjoy writing, be able to write well, and be able to express your ideas and those of others clearly. You should learn all about the English language and work hard on your grammar and spelling skills. You should be curious, enjoy learning about new things, and have an interest in science or medicine.

DID YOU KNOW?

Where Science and Medical Writers Work

- Newspapers and magazines
- Medical publishers
- Pharmaceutical and drug companies
- Medical research institutions
- Government agencies
- Insurance companies
- Nonprofit organizations
- Medical and scientific associations
- Self-employment

Education and Training

If you are considering a career as a writer, you should take as many English and writing classes as you can. Computer classes will also be helpful. If you know in high school that you want to do scientific or medical writing, you should take biology, physiology, chemistry, physics, math, health, and other science courses.

Not all writers go to college, but today's employers almost always require applicants to have a bachelor's degree. Many writers earn an undergraduate degree in English, journalism, or liberal arts and then obtain a master's degree in a communications field such as medical or science writing.

FOR MORE INFO

For information on a career as a medical writer, contact
American Medical Writers Association
30 West Gude Drive, Suite 525
Rockville, MD 20850-1161
301-294-5303
amwa@amwa.org
http://www.amwa.org

To read advice for beginning science writers, visit the association's Web site.
National Association of Science Writers
PO Box 7905
Berkeley, CA 94707-0905

510-647-9500
http://www.nasw.org

For information on careers in technical communication, contact
Society for Technical Communication
9401 Lee Highway, Suite 300
Fairfax, VA 22031-1803
703-522-4114
stc@stc.org
http://www.stc.org

Earnings

There are no specific salary studies for science and medical writers. The U.S. Department of Labor reports that all writers earned salaries that ranged from less than $28,000 to more than $106,000 in 2008. Writers who worked for newspaper, periodical, book, and directory publishers earned mean salaries of about $52,000.

Outlook

There is a lot of competition for writing jobs, and only the most talented and hardworking writers will be able to land jobs. As we see more advances in medicine and science, there will continue to be a need for skilled writers to provide that information to the public and professionals. Those with master's degrees in medical or science writing will have the best employment prospects.

Science Technicians

What Science Technicians Do

Science technicians help scientists, engineers, and researchers solve problems and invent new processes and products. They work in a variety of fields, but the one common trait that they share is that they help people live better lives.

The following paragraphs provide an overview of the most popular specialties for science technicians.

Agricultural technicians help engineers, scientists, and conservationists in food, plant, soil, and animal research, production, and processing. *Agribusiness technicians* combine their agriculture and business backgrounds to manage or offer management consulting services to farms and agricultural businesses.

Biological technicians assist biological scientists. They often work in teams on laboratory experiments. Many biological technicians work in medical research—helping to find a cure for AIDS or multiple sclerosis or to develop medicines.

Chemical technicians conduct physical tests, chemical analyses, and instrumental analyses for research, product development, quality control, and establishing standards.

Engineering technicians assist engineers, scientists, and other workers in a variety of tasks. They are highly trained workers with

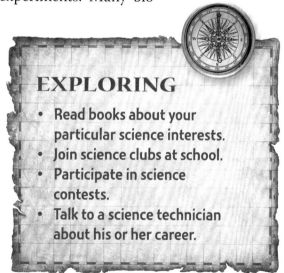

EXPLORING

- Read books about your particular science interests.
- Join science clubs at school.
- Participate in science contests.
- Talk to a science technician about his or her career.

A biological science technician records water depth measurements. (Scott Bauer, USDA, Agricultural Research Service)

strong backgrounds in a specialized technological field, such as aerospace, civil, materials, and many other types of engineering.

Environmental technicians, also known as *pollution control technicians,* conduct tests and field investigations to obtain soil samples and other data. Their research is used by engineers, scientists, and others who help clean up, monitor, control, or prevent pollution. An environmental technician usually specializes in air, water, or soil pollution. A small number specialize in noise pollution.

Tips for Success

To be a successful science technician, you should

- enjoy science
- be curious
- be very accurate in your work
- have excellent communication skills
- always be on time for work
- be able to follow instructions
- be willing to continue to learn throughout your career
- be able to work independently and as part of a team
- be willing to work irregular hours when necessary

Forensic science technicians, also known as *forensic technicians,* help forensic scientists analyze, identify, and classify physical evidence relating to criminal cases. They may work in laboratories or they may travel to crime scenes to collect evidence.

Forestry technicians help plan, supervise, and conduct operations necessary to maintain and protect forests. They also manage forests and wildlife areas, control fires, insects, and disease and limit the depletion (loss) of forest resources.

Geological technicians assist geologists and engineers by gathering, plotting, and storing samples and technical data. Geological technicians work in the field of the geosciences. Geosciences are the sciences dealing with the Earth, including geology, geophysics, and geochemistry. Usually, they work under the supervision of a geologist or geoscientist who is trained to study the Earth's physical makeup and history. Often, geoscientists spe-

DID YOU KNOW?

Where Science Technicians Work

- Colleges and universities
- Self employment
- U.S. military
- State and local government agencies
- Private companies (pharmaceutical companies, hospitals, biotechnology companies, and laboratories)
- Federal government agencies (such as U.S. Departments of Departments of Agriculture, Commerce, Energy, Health and Human Services, and Interior; Environmental Protection Agency)

cialize in one area of study. Among these specialties are environmental geology, the study of how pollution, waste, and hazardous material affect the Earth and its features; geophysics, the study of the Earth's interior and magnetic, electric, and gravitational fields; hydrology, the investigation of the movement and quality of surface water; petroleum geology, the exploration and production of crude oil and natural gas; and seismology, the study of earthquakes and the forces that cause them.

Nuclear technicians, also known as *radiation protection technicians,* monitor radiation levels, protect workers, and decontaminate (clean up) radioactive areas. They work under the supervision of nuclear scientists, engineers, or power plant managers. They are trained to detect, measure, and identify different kinds of nuclear radiation. They know federal regulations and allowable levels of radiation. Technicians who control nuclear reactors are known as *nuclear reactor operators.*

Petroleum technicians assist in the exploration of petroleum (crude oil) fields and in the production of oil and gas. They test potential sources, drill test wells, improve drilling technology, collect petroleum from producing wells, and deliver oil to pipelines.

Seismic technicians help seismologists gather data so they can better understand and predict earthquakes and other vibrations of the Earth. Seismic technicians use seismographs and other geophysical instruments to collect and analyze data.

Soil conservation technicians develop soil conservation plans for landowners, such as farmers and ranchers. They help preserve the Earth's natural resources: soil, water, wildlife, crops, and forests.

Education and Training

In high school, take courses in mathematics, science, computer science, English, and speech to give yourself a good general preparation for the field. If you've already picked a particular career path, it is a good idea to take classes in that area. For example, if you want to become a chemical technician, you should take chemistry classes. If you want to work as an environmental technician, take classes in environmental science, botany, zoology, and ecology. If you think a career as a forensic technician is in your future, take forensic science, chemistry, and related classes.

Most science technician positions require an associate's degree or a certificate in applied science or science-related technology. Biological technicians and forensic science technicians need a bachelor's degree. Some technicians enter the field with only a high school diploma and receive extensive on-the-job training before eventually earning a two-year degree.

Earnings

Salaries also vary according to geographic location, experience, and education. The U.S. Department of Labor reports the following median annual earnings for science technicians in 2008 by specialty: agricultural and food science technicians, $33,990; biological technicians, $38,400; chemical technicians, $42,120; environmental science and protection technicians, including health, $40,230; forensic science technicians, $49,860; forest and conservation technicians, $32,000; geological and petroleum technicians, $53,360; and nuclear technicians, $67,890. Salaries for science technicians ranged from less than $22,000 to $97,000 or more. In general, technicians working in remote areas and under severe weather conditions usually receive higher rates of pay, as do technicians who work at large companies and companies with union workers.

FOR MORE INFO

For general information about chemistry careers and education programs, contact

American Chemical Society
1155 16th Street, NW
Washington, DC 20036-4839
800-227-5558
http://www.chemistry.org

For information on geoscience careers, contact

American Geological Institute
4220 King Street
Alexandria, VA 22302-1502
703-379-2480
http://www.agiweb.org

For information about career options in biology, contact

American Institute of Biological Sciences
1444 I Street, NW, Suite 200
Washington, DC 20005-6535

202-628-1500
http://www.aibs.org

To learn more about careers, contact

American Society of Agricultural and Biological Engineers
2950 Niles Road
St. Joseph, MI 49085-8607
269-429-0300
hq@asabe.org
http://www.asae.org

For information about careers in biotechnology, contact

Biotechnology Industry Organization
1201 Maryland Avenue, SW, Suite 900
Washington, DC 20024-2149
202-962-9200
info@bio.org
http://www.bio.org

Outlook

Employment of science technicians is expected to be good during the next decade—although the employment outlook varies by career specialty. For example, employment for chemical technicians is not expected to grow much, while there should be some employment growth for forestry and conservation, agricultural, and nuclear technicians. Strong employment is expected for biological technicians. There will be excellent job growth for forensic science technicians and environmental science and protection technicians.

Soil Scientists

What Soil Scientists Do

To use soil wisely and keep it from washing away or being damaged, experts must analyze, or study, it and find the best ways to manage it. *Soil scientists* are these experts. Soil scientists collect soil samples and study their chemical and physical characteristics. They study how soil responds to fertilizers and various kinds of farming practices. This helps farmers decide what types of crops to grow on certain soils.

Soil scientists often work outdoors. They go to fields to take soil samples. They spend many hours meeting with farmers and discussing ways to avoid soil damage. They may suggest that a farmer grow crops on different parts of a farm every few years so that the unused soil can recover. Soil scientists may also recommend that a farmer use various fertilizers to put nutrients back into the soil. They may suggest ways to protect the crops to keep the wind from blowing the soil away.

EXPLORING

- Visit the following Web sites to learn more about soil and soil conservation: Dig It!: The Secrets of Soil (http://forces.si.edu/soils), Underground Adventure (http://www.fieldmuseum.org/undergroundadventure), and Just for Kids: Soil Biological Communities (http://www.blm.gov/nstc/soil/Kids).
- Join a chapter of the National 4-H Council (http://www.fourhcouncil.edu) or National FFA Organization (http://www.ffa.org).
- Look for part-time or summer work on a farm or ranch.
- Ask your teacher or counselor to arrange an interview with a soil scientist.

Soil scientists work for agricultural research laboratories, crop production companies, and other organizations. They also work with road departments to advise them about the quality and condition of the soil over which roads will be built.

Some soil scientists travel to foreign countries to conduct research and learn how other scientists treat the soil. Many also teach at colleges, universities, and agricultural schools.

Soil scientists must be able to work on their own and with other scientists and technicians. They must be willing to spend many hours outdoors in all kinds of weather. Soil scientists should be detail oriented in order to do accurate research, and they should enjoy solving problems. Soil scientists should be

A soil scientist studies data used in a greenhouse study. (Stephen Ausmus, USDA, Agricultural Research Service)

Words to Learn

aeration porosity the fraction of the volume of soil that is filled with air at any given time

blowout a small area from which soil material has been removed by wind

creep slow mass movement of soil and soil material down steep slopes; creep is primarily caused by gravity, but aided by saturation with water and by alternate freezing and thawing

erosion the wearing away of soil and other land features by water, wind, and human activities, such as farming and construction

fertilizer natural and chemical elements that help plants to grow; chemical fertilizers can be harmful if used in too large quantities

macronutrient a nutrient found in high amounts in plants

nutrient a substance that encourages growth

peat a mixture of decaying plant matter

scarp a cliff or steep slope along the edge of a plateau

organized and effective time managers. They should be comfortable using technology such as computers. They should not mind getting dirty while conducting research in the field.

Education and Training

To be a soil scientist, you need a solid background in mathematics and science, especially the physical and earth sciences.

The best way to become a soil scientist is to go to college and earn a bachelor's degree. Then you should go on to earn a master's degree in agricultural or soil science. Typical classes for soil science majors include statistics, mathematics, general soils, soil morphology/classification/mapping, soil physics, soil chemistry, soil biology, soil fertility, and technical writing. A degree in biology, physics, or chemistry might also be accept-

DID YOU KNOW?

Here is a list of creatures that live below ground (at least some of the time) and details on the role they play in the food web:

- Burrowing animals (such as prairie dogs, ground squirrels, badgers, owls, snakes, lizards, and rabbits) dig holes that mix up the soil and allow water to reach plants. These holes also allow water to drain and reduce flooding.
- Arthropods (such as ants, termites, and spiders) break up the soil, which allows air into the soil that helps plants grow. They chew up dead plants into small pieces that can be broken down more easily by fungi and bacteria. Arthropods also serve as food for larger soil dwellers.
- Nematodes are tiny roundworms that live in grassy soils. Some are harmful to plants, but others provide food for plants.
- Protozoa are tiny organisms that eat bacteria. When they eat bacteria, nitrogen and other nutrients (plant food) are released for plants to eat.
- Bacteria are one-celled organisms. They are so tiny that you need a microscope to see them. They make food for plants.
- Fungi are non-green plants. Some grow on plant roots and help them to get food and water. Others form mushrooms and help decompose dead plants.
- Biological soil crusts are tiny communities of bacteria and living plants. They live just above or below the surface. They hold the soil together so it doesn't blow or wash away. They make plant food and keep out weeds.

Source: Bureau of Land Management

able, but you should take some courses in agriculture. With a bachelor's degree in agricultural science, you can get some non-research jobs, but you will not be able to advance very far. Most research and teaching positions require a doctorate.

Earnings

According to the U.S. Department of Labor, average earnings for soil and plant scientists were $58,390 in 2008. Workers who were just starting out made $34,000 or less. Soil and plant

FOR MORE INFO

For information on agricultural careers, contact
American Society of Agronomy
5585 Guilford Road
Madison, WI 53711-5801
608-273-8080
headquarters@Agronomy.org
http://www.agronomy.org

For information on educational institutions that offer soil science programs, contact
National Society of Consulting Soil Scientists
PO Box 1219
Sandpoint, ID 83864-0860
800-535-7148
http://www.nscss.org

Contact the NRCS for information on government soil conservation careers. Its Web site has information on becoming an Earth Team volunteer.

Natural Resources Conservation Service (NRCS)
U.S. Department of Agriculture
1400 Independence Avenue, SW
Washington, DC 20250-0002
http://www.nrcs.usda.gov

For information on soil conservation and publications, contact
Soil and Water Conservation Society
945 SW Ankeny Road
Ankeny, IA 50023-9723
515-289-2331
http://www.swcs.org

To read "Soils Sustain Life," visit the society's Web site.
Soil Science Society of America
5585 Guilford Road
Madison, WI 53711-5801
608-273-8080
http://www.soils.org

scientists with a lot of experience earned more than $105,000. Salaries for soil scientists who work for the federal government are higher. In 2009, they had average earnings of $79,158 a year.

Outlook

Soil scientists should find plenty of job opportunities during the next decade. They will be needed to help improve soil fertility, reduce erosion, and clean up polluted soil, among other responsibilities. Additionally, there have not been as many agricultural students in the past few years as there once were. This will create more job openings.

Zoologists

What Zoologists Do

Zoologists are biologists who study animals. They usually specialize in one animal group. *Entomologists* are experts on insects. *Ornithologists* study birds. *Mammalogists* focus on mammals. *Herpetologists* specialize in reptiles. *Ichthyologists* study fish.

Some zoologists specialize even more. They focus on a specific part or aspect of an animal. For example, a zoologist might study single-celled organisms, a particular variety of fish (such as the Black Diamond Gold Piranha), or the behavior of one group of animals, such as ocelots, owls, or orangutans.

Some zoologists are primarily teachers. Others spend most of their time doing research. Nearly all zoologists spend a major portion of their time at the computer. Most zoologists spend very little time outdoors (an average of two to eight weeks per year). In fact, junior scientists often spend more time in the field than senior scientists do. Senior scientists coordinate research, supervise other workers, and try to find funding. Raising money is an extremely important activity for zoologists who work for government agencies or universities. They need the money to pay for research and fieldwork.

Basic research zoologists conduct experiments on live or dead animals, in a laboratory or in natural surroundings. They make discoveries that might help humans. Such research in the past has led to discoveries about nutrition, aging, food production, and pest control. Some research zoologists work in the field with wild animals, such as bobcats or bears. They trace their movements with radio transmitters and observe their eat-

EXPLORING

- Watch nature shows on television.
- Learn as much as you can about animals on the Internet. Here are a few Web site suggestions: Animal Corner (http://www.animalcorner.co.uk), Oakland Zoo: Animals (http://www.oaklandzoo.org/animals), and Yahoo! Kids: Animals (http://kids.yahoo.com/animals).
- Read books and other publications about animals. Here are a few book suggestions: *Endangered Animals,* by Rhonda Lucas Donald (Children's Press, 2001); *National Geographic Encyclopedia of Animals,* by Karen McGhee and George McKay (National Geographic Children's Books, 2007); and *Wild Science: Amazing Encounters Between Animals and the People Who Study Them,* by Victoria Miles, Martin Kratt, and Chris Kratt (Raincoast Books, 2004).
- Volunteer at your local zoo or aquarium.
- Ask your school librarian to help you find books and videos on animals and animal behavior.
- Explore hobbies such as bird-watching, insect collecting, or raising hamsters, rabbits, and other pets.
- Offer to pet sit for your neighbors. This will give you a chance to observe and care for animals.
- Interview a zoologist about his or her career.

ing habits, mating patterns, and other behavior. Researchers use all kinds of laboratory chemicals and equipment such as dissecting tools, microscopes, slides, electron microscopes, and other complicated machinery.

Zoologists in applied research use basic research to solve problems in medicine, conservation, and aquarium and zoo

DID YOU KNOW?

Where Zoologists Work

- Zoos
- Aquariums
- Museums
- Colleges and universities
- Nonprofit organizations
- Government agencies

work. For example, applied researchers may develop a new drug for people or animals. Others may invent a new pesticide or a new type of pet food. (A pesticide is a substance, often made from chemicals, that is used to stop a pest—an animal, insect, or other organism—from hurting plants or animals.)

Many zoologists teach in colleges and universities while they do their own research. Some zoologists manage zoos and aquariums. Still others work for government agencies, private businesses, and research organizations.

Education and Training

Science classes, especially in biology, are important if you want to become a zoologist. You should also study English, communications, and computer science.

After high school, you must go to college to earn a bachelor's degree. A master's or doctoral degree is usually also required. You do not need to choose a particular major until you enter a master's degree program.

Earnings

Zoologists earned average salaries of $55,290 a year in 2008, according to the U.S. Department of Labor (DOL). The most experienced zoologists earned more than $91,000. Beginning salaries for those with a bachelor's degree in biological and life sciences were $33,254 in July 2009, according to the National Association of Colleges and Employers. Zoologists who worked for the federal government earned average salaries of about $116,908 in 2009, according to the DOL.

Profile: Jane Goodall (1934–   )

Jane Goodall is a world-famous primatologist, anthropologist, and animal advocate. She is best known for her work studying and protecting chimpanzees in Tanzania in Africa. Goodall's love of chimpanzees started when she was two years old. Her father gave her a lifelike toy chimpanzee named Jubilee. People thought the toy might scare her, but she loved it. Goodall still keeps Jubilee in her home today.

Around the age of 10 or 11, Goodall told her parents that she wanted to go to Africa to live with and study chimpanzees and other animals. At the time, young women were not encouraged to pursue most careers. But Goodall's mother strongly urged her to follow her dreams.

At age 23, Goodall made her first trip to Kenya in Africa. During this trip, she met Dr. Louis Leakey, a well-known paleontologist and anthropologist. He was impressed by her knowledge of Africa and wildlife, and he hired her as his assistant. Goodall helped him search for and study fossils (evidence of ancient life), and then worked at a museum in Kenya.

Jane liked this work but really wanted to study live animals, not fossils. Dr. Leakey suggested she study chimpanzees that lived near Lake Tanganyika in East Africa (now Tanzania). Goodall thought this was a great idea.

It took some work, though, to convince the British authorities (who governed this area of Africa at the time) to allow her to go. They didn't think a young woman should be living in the African wilderness surrounded by wild animals.

The authorities finally agreed to allow Goodall to go to Tanganyika, but only if her mother stayed with her for the first three months! In the summer of 1960, she and her mother arrived at Gombe National Park in Tanganyika.

At first, studying the chimpanzees was a challenge. They were afraid and ran away from her. They weren't used to a human living in their midst. With time and determination, Goodall gradually gained their trust. She began making amazing discoveries that changed the way people think about chimpanzees and animals in general. She discovered that chimpanzees made and used tools to hunt for termites. Before this, it was thought that only humans could make tools. She also found that chimpanzees had unique personalities and that they ate meat (many thought chimpanzees ate only plants).

Today, Jane Goodall continues her work with the chimpanzees of Gombe via the Jane Goodall Institute for Wildlife Research, Education and Conservation. She travels the world to educate people about chimpanzees and conservation. Visit http://www.janegoodall.org/jane to learn more about Jane Goodall.

FOR MORE INFO

For information about a career as a zoologist, contact
American Institute of Biological Sciences
1444 I Street, NW, Suite 200
Washington, DC 20005-6535
202-628-1500
http://www.aibs.org

For information on membership, a list of accredited zoos throughout the world, and careers in aquatic and marine science, contact
Association of Zoos and Aquariums
8403 Colesville Road, Suite 710
Silver Spring, MD 20910-3314
301-562-0777
http://www.aza.org

For information about all areas of zoology, contact

Society for Integrative and Comparative Biology
1313 Dolley Madison Boulevard, Suite 402
McLean, VA 22101-3926
800-955-1236
http://www.sicb.org

The association "promotes conservation, preservation, and propagation of animals in both private and public domains." It offers a membership category for those who support its goals.
Zoological Association of America
PO Box 511275
Punta Gorda, FL 33951-1275
813-449-4356
info@zaa.org
http://www.zaa.org

Outlook

Employment for zoologists is expected to be good in coming years. This is because there is increasing interest in protecting and studying animals. But since this field is small, there will be a lot of competition for research jobs. Zoologists with advanced degrees and years of research experience in their specialty will enjoy the best job prospects.

Glossary

accredited approved as meeting established standards for providing good training and education; this approval is usually given by an independent organization of professionals

annual salary the money an individual earns for an entire year of work

apprentice a person who is learning a trade by working under the supervision of a skilled worker; apprentices often receive classroom instruction in addition to their supervised practical experience

associate's degree an academic rank or title granted by a community college, junior college, or similar institution to graduates of a two-year program of education beyond high school

bachelor's degree an academic rank or title given to a person who has completed a four-year program of study at a college or university; also called an **undergraduate degree** or **baccalaureate**

career an occupation for which a worker receives training and has an opportunity for advancement

certified approved as meeting established requirements for skill, knowledge, and experience in a particular field; people are certified by an organization of professionals in their field

college a higher education institution that is above the high school level

community college a public or private two-year college attended by students who do not usually live at the college; graduates of a community college receive an associate's degree and may transfer to a four-year college or university to complete a bachelor's degree

diploma a certificate or document given by a school to show that a person has completed a course or has graduated from the school

distance education a type of educational program that allows students to take classes and complete their education by mail or the Internet

doctorate   the highest academic rank or title granted by a graduate school to a person who has completed a two- to three-year program after having received a master's degree

fellowship   a financial award given for research projects or dissertation assistance; fellowships are commonly offered at the graduate, postgraduate, or doctoral levels

freelancer   a worker who is not a regular employee of a company; freelancers work for themselves and do not receive a regular paycheck

fringe benefit   a payment or benefit to an employee in addition to regular wages or salary; examples of fringe benefits include a pension, a paid vacation, and health or life insurance

graduate school   a school that people may attend after they have received their bachelor's degree; people who complete an educational program at a graduate school earn a master's degree or a doctorate

intern   an advanced student (usually one with at least some college training) in a professional field who is employed in a job that is intended to provide supervised practical experience for the student

internship   1. the position or job of an intern; 2. the period of time when a person is an intern

junior college   a two-year college that offers courses like those in the first half of a four-year college program; graduates of a junior college usually receive an associate's degree and may transfer to a four-year college or university to complete a bachelor's degree

liberal arts   the subjects covered by college courses that develop broad general knowledge rather than specific occupational skills; the liberal arts are often considered to include philosophy, literature and language, the arts, history, and some courses in the social sciences and natural sciences

major (in college)   the academic field in which a student specializes and receives a degree

master's degree   an academic rank or title granted by a graduate school to a person who has completed a one- or two-year program after earning a bachelor's degree

medical degree   a degree awarded to an individual who has completed four years of training at a medical school

medical school   a school that students attend in order to become a physician; people who complete an educational program at a medical school earn either a doctor of medicine (M.D.) or osteopathic medicine (D.O.) degree

pension   an amount of money paid regularly by an employer to a former employee after he or she retires from working

scholarship   A gift of money to a student to help the student pay for further education

social studies   courses of study (such as civics, geography, and history) that deal with how human societies work

starting salary   salary paid to a newly hired employee; the starting salary is usually a smaller amount than is paid to a more experienced worker

technical college   a private or public college offering two- or four-year programs in technical subjects; technical colleges offer courses in both general and technical subjects and award associate's degrees and bachelor's degrees

undergraduate   a student at a college or university who has not yet received a degree

undergraduate degree   see **bachelor's degree**

union   an organization whose members are workers in a particular industry or company; the union works to gain better wages, benefits, and working conditions for its members; also called a **labor union** or **trade union**

vocational school   a public or private school that offers training in one or more skills or trades

wage   money that is paid in return for work done, especially money paid on the basis of the number of hours or days worked

Browse and Learn More

Books

Burnett, Rebecca. *Careers for Number Crunchers & Other Quantitative Types.* 2d ed. New York: McGraw-Hill, 2002.

Claverie, Jean-Michel, and Cedric Notredame. *Bioinformatics For Dummies.* 2d ed. Hoboken, N.J.: For Dummies, 2006.

Clemens, Meg, Glenn Clemens, and Sean Clemens. *The Everything Kids' Math Puzzles Book: Brain Teasers, Games, and Activities for Hours of Fun.* Cincinnati: Adams Media Corporation, 2003.

Dingle, Adrian. *The Periodic Table: Elements with Style!* New York: Kingfisher, 2007.

Eberts, Marjorie. *Careers for Computer Buffs & Other Technological Types.* 3d ed. New York: McGraw-Hill, 2006.

Enzensberger, Hans Magnus, Rotraut Susanne Berner, and Michael Henry Heim. *The Number Devil: A Mathematical Adventure.* New York: Holt Paperbacks, 2000.

Fitzgerald, Theresa R. *Math Dictionary for Kids: The Essential Guide to Math Terms, Strategies, and Tables.* Waco, Tex.: Prufrock Press, 2005.

Gralla, Preston. *How the Internet Works.* 8th ed. Indianapolis: Que Publishing, 2006.

Green, Dan. *Astronomy: Out of This World!* New York: Kingfisher, 2009.

———. *Math: A Book You Can Count On.* New York: Kingfisher, 2010.

———. *Physics: Why Matter Matters!* New York: Kingfisher, 2008.

———. *Planet Earth: What Planet Are You On?* New York: Kingfisher, 2010.

Hawking, Stephen, and Lucy Hawking. *George's Cosmic Treasure Hunt.* New York: Simon & Schuster Children's Publishing, 2009.

———. *George's Secret Key to the Universe.* New York: Simon & Schuster Children's Publishing, 2009.

Ishikawa, Kenji. *The Manga Guide to the Universe.* San Francisco: No Starch Press, 2010.

Kojima, Hiroyuki. *The Manga Guide to Calculus.* San Francisco: No Starch Press, 2009.

Kraynak, Joe. *The Complete Idiot's Guide to Computer Basics.* 5th ed. New York: Alpha, 2009.

Long, Lynette. *Math Smarts: Tips, Tricks, and Secrets for Making Math More Fun!* Middleton, Wisc.: American Girl Publishing, 2004.

Miller, Michael. *Absolute Beginner's Guide to Computer Basics.* 5th ed. Indianapolis: Que Publishing, 2009.

Nitta, Hideo, and Keita Takatsu. *The Manga Guide to Physics.* San Francisco: No Starch Press, 2009.

Salvadori, Mario. *The Art of Construction: Projects and Principles for Beginning Engineers and Architects.* 3d ed. Chicago: Chicago Review Press, 2000.

Takahashi, Shin. *The Manga Guide to Statistics.* San Francisco: No Starch Press, 2008.

VanCleave, Janice. *Janice VanCleave's Engineering for Every Kid: Easy Activities That Make Learning Science Fun.* Hoboken, N.J.: Wiley, 2007.

Walker, Jearl. *Flying Circus of Physics.* 2d ed. Hoboken, N.J.: Wiley, 2006.

White, Ron, and Timothy Edward Downs. *How Computers Work.* 9th ed. Indianapolis: Que Publishing, 2007.

Woods, Michael, and Mary B. Woods. *Ancient Machines: From Wedges to Waterwheels.* Minneapolis: Runestone Press, 1999.

Periodicals

Astronomy
http://www.astronomy.com

eGFI: Dream Up the Future
http://www.egfi-k12.org/read-the-magazine

PhysicsQuest
http://www.physicscentral.com/physicsquest

Plus Magazine
http://plus.maths.org

The Pre-Engineering Times
http://www.jets.org/publications/petimes.cfm

Time for Kids
http://www.timeforkids.com/TFK

Web Sites

A+ Math
http://www.aplusmath.com

AAA Math
http://www.aaamath.com

Accounting for Kids
http://www.accountingforkids.com

American Library Association: Great Web Sites for Kids
http://www.ala.org/greatsites

ARCHcareers.org
http://www.archcareers.org

Ask Dr. Math
http://mathforum.org/dr.math/dr-math.html

Ask the Space Scientist
http://image.gsfc.nasa.gov/poetry/ask/askmag.html

Astronomy Today
http://www.astronomytoday.com

Be a Math Teacher
http://www.nctm.org/resources/content.aspx?id=530

Careers in Optics
http://spie.org/x30120.xml

Computer History Museum
http://www.computerhistory.org

Computing Degrees and Careers
http://computingcareers.acm.org

CoolMath.com
http://coolmath.com

eGFI: Dream Up the Future
http://egfi-k12.org

Engineer Girl!
http://www.engineergirl.org

Exploring the Science of Light!
http://www.opticsforteens.org

Fermilab: Education
http://www.fnal.gov/pub/education/k-12_programs.html

Frank Potter's Science Gems: Mathematics
http://sciencegems.com/math.html

Free On-Line Dictionary of Computing
http://foldoc.org

Indexes of Biographies (Mathematicians)
http://www-groups.dcs.st-and.ac.uk/~history/BiogIndex.html

Intro to Astronomy
http://www.astronomy.com/asy/default.aspx?c=ps&id=6

Invention Dimension
http://web.mit.edu/invent/invent-main.html

Light in Action: Lasers, Cameras & Other Cool Stuff
http://spie.org/x30120.xml

Math Cats
http://www.mathcats.com

Math Is Fun
http://www.mathsisfun.com

Math Playground
http://www.MathPlayground.com

Math Words
http://www.mathwords.com/a_to_z.htm

MinyanLand
http://www.minyanland.com

National Aeronautics and Space Administration: For Students Grades K–4
http://www.nasa.gov/audience/forstudents/k-4

National Aeronautics and Space Administration: For Students Grades 5–8
http://www.nasa.gov/audience/forstudents/5-8

National Inventors Hall of Fame
http://www.invent.org/hall_of_fame/1_0_0_hall_of_fame.asp

A New Universe to Discover: Careers in Astronomy
http://aas.org/education/careers.php

Operations Research: The Science of Better
http://www.scienceofbetter.org

Optics: Light at Work
http://spie.org/x30120.xml

PhysicsCentral
http://www.physicscentral.com

Physics Students
http://www.aps.org/careers/student

A Sightseer's Guide to Engineering
http://www.engineeringsights.org

Society of Exploration Geophysicists Kids
http://students.seg.org/kids

SpaceWeather.com
http://www.spaceweather.com

Start Here, Go Places
http://www.startheregoplaces.com

The Tech Museum of Innovation
http://www.thetech.org

Thinking of a Career in Applied Mathematics?
http://www.siam.org/careers/thinking.php

U.S. Department of Energy: For Students and Kids
http://www.energy.gov/forstudentsandkids.htm

Why Choose Computer Science & Engineering?
http://www.cs.washington.edu/WhyCSE

Index